For Jan
with my best wishes.
Sue Rengelly

SATNAV FOR YOUR SOUL

*Guidance from Those Who Have
Made the Ultimate Journey*

SUSAN PENGELLY

BALBOA
PRESS
A DIVISION OF HAY HOUSE

Copyright © 2013 Susan Pengelly.

All rights reserved. No part of this book may be used or reproduced by any means, graphic, electronic, or mechanical, including photocopying, recording, taping or by any information storage retrieval system without the written permission of the publisher except in the case of brief quotations embodied in critical articles and reviews.

Balboa Press books may be ordered through booksellers or by contacting:

Balboa Press
A Division of Hay House
1663 Liberty Drive
Bloomington, IN 47403
www.balboapress.com
1 (877) 407-4847

Because of the dynamic nature of the Internet, any web addresses or links contained in this book may have changed since publication and may no longer be valid. The views expressed in this work are solely those of the author and do not necessarily reflect the views of the publisher, and the publisher hereby disclaims any responsibility for them.

The author of this book does not dispense medical advice or prescribe the use of any technique as a form of treatment for physical, emotional, or medical problems without the advice of a physician, either directly or indirectly. The intent of the author is only to offer information of a general nature to help you in your quest for emotional and spiritual well-being. In the event you use any of the information in this book for yourself, which is your constitutional right, the author and the publisher assume no responsibility for your actions.

Cover Photograph by Laura Yeo

Any people depicted in stock imagery provided by Thinkstock are models, and such images are being used for illustrative purposes only.
Certain stock imagery © Thinkstock.

Printed in the United States of America.

ISBN: 978-1-4525-8460-7 (sc)
ISBN: 978-1-4525-8461-4 (hc)
ISBN: 978-1-4525-8459-1 (e)

Library of Congress Control Number: 2013918458

Balboa Press rev. date: 11/05/2013

*I dedicate this book to all the people I have ever communicated with
Who are a little further along the path . . .
thank you for trusting me with your stories.*

*To my husband Stephen, my children Claire, Sarah, Laura and Tom
and my grandchildren, who light up my life from the inside.*

*To my dearest friends, you know who you are, especially Pam and Dawn,
You all add immeasurably to my life by standing
by me no matter what and loving me,
I am the person I am because of you all.
Thank you.*

*And also to you, the reader, because these stories, each one a seed,
will plant themselves in your consciousness
And you will forever know that death is not the end of love.*

Contents

Foreword ix
Preface xi
Introduction xv

Part I: The Monologues

Chapter 1:   Mark 1
Chapter 2:   Frannie 6
Chapter 3:   Robert 10
Chapter 4:   Tony 15
Chapter 5:   Arthur 19
Chapter 6:   Danny 25
Chapter 7:   Rosemarie 28
Chapter 8:   Sharon 33
Chapter 9:   Iris 37
Chapter 10: Harold 41
Chapter 11: Gwen 43
Chapter 12: Alma 47
Chapter 13: Billy Boy 52
Chapter 14: Ethan 55
Chapter 15: Brenda 60
Chapter 16: Jon 67
Chapter 17: Bridget 71
Chapter 18: Lisle 78
Chapter 19: Betty 81
Chapter 20: Jake 84

Chapter 21: Liam 87
Chapter 22: Valerie 91
Chapter 23: Iain 94
Chapter 24: Karis 98
Chapter 25: Chris 102
Chapter 26: Gavin 105
Chapter 27: Edwin 111
Chapter 28: Sonia 115
Chapter 29: Evan 119
Chapter 30: Mal 121
Chapter 31: Billy 123
Chapter 32: Adam 127
Chapter 33: Julie 131
Chapter 34: Edward 136
Chapter 35: Dementia 140
Chapter 36: Marnie 142
Chapter 37: Existence 146
Chapter 38: Heaven & Hell 147

Part II: My Life

Chapter 39 153
Chapter 40 159
Chapter 41 161
Chapter 42 168
Chapter 43 171
Chapter 44 173
Chapter 45 177
Chapter 46 180
Chapter 47 185
Chapter 48 187
Chapter 49 191

About the Author 195

Foreword

I first met Sue in the mid 90's. I had been 'drawn in' to the spiritual side of life in 1990 when my home somehow became a 'poltergeist's playground', where New Agers from Glastonbury, Totnes, St. Ives and beyond held frequent workshops. When Sue first opened her door to me I was taken aback. I had been used to the rainbow-clothed reincarnations of King Arthur, Guinevere and Henry VIII. Sue was the polar opposite.

I'd met some excellent channellers, tarot readers, healers and the rest, but Sue was in a different league. She immediately started telling me things about myself, such as the relationship I had with my parents, and the specific people I had at Tapeley (my home) who I needed to keep an eye on.

Since then I've attended a few of Sue's clairvoyance classes where she helped me to open up to new (for me) aspects of the Spiritual side of life. However, more importantly for me, Sue has helped free many trapped spirits in my house and friend's houses.

This might sound 'wishy washy' to many people but we have an area at Tapeley called 'Jacob's ladder' which was the servants quarters in the 1800's. The room on the far left has always had an atmosphere and no guests or residents ever felt comfortable staying there. One day when I came back from the shops a lady who had organised jousting at Tapeley was outside the backdoor. As soon as I got out of my car she started ranting at me like some crazy lunatic. I asked what she had been doing and she said she had been cleaning the room in question in Jacob's Ladder and had been very frightened by someone in there. There was only one person I knew who could possibly sort this problem out.

A week or so later, I went into the room with Sue and my head immediately scrambled with confusion and anxiety as usual. Sue calmly spoke to the (what was a) young girl who had been murdered in the mid 1800's and was deeply upset that no one would listen to her story. Sue gently told her that she had been dwelling on this for quite long enough and it was now time to calm down and she would listen. Susan spent some time doing this and then told the girl that she would help her to be with all the people she had loved who were waiting for her. At the exact moment Susan did this the whole energy changed in the room, and folk are now sleeping there in peace.

Many people in the local area will have similar stories. Sue is a quite extraordinary lady with a strength and self-assurance that nothing will 'go wrong' (and nothing does) and has helped a great many physical and non physical people.

Hector Christie

Books written by Hector Christie:-

No Blade of Grass (is blown without divine intention)
The Final Curtain Call

PREFACE

Well, you have obviously picked up *this* book for a reason and I'll lay odds it's because you have 'lost' someone you love. Isn't that an odd term? Lost? It makes it sound as though you've carelessly left them somewhere. People you love who have left this physical world are not 'lost' to you. That is such a lonely word. They are not wandering in the ether trying to find their way to somewhere they should be. No, the people you love who are no longer physically here—and let's face it, that's the painful part, the physical loss of their presence in your life—they are not very far away, not very far at all.

In fact, the people you love and who love you are only a thought away. That's the key you see—thought. You know when your grandmother comes to mind for no reason at all? That's because she is thinking of *you*. All communication between those who have passed from this world and you is a thought. Thought loaded with love. Emotional content is the key to *all* communication. Come to think of it, that's just as important in this physical world, if there was more of it there would be fewer wars but that's a whole different book.

I 'know' all this from many years of experience; over thirty five years in fact, of interacting with what we know as 'dead' people. That alone is enough to give most people the heebie-jeebies but to me . . . to me it's as normal as breathing.

I became aware of hearing and seeing the occasional 'dead' person when I was coming up to eleven. This has never scared me, and over the years, I have had my life saved several times because of it. I figured anything that went to the trouble to save me from myself or others was never going to hurt me, and so the ability to 'know things' progressed.

It's not weird . . . it's nothing to do with the occult which only means the unknown, but the less well informed trot this term out in the hope that it sounds scary enough to stop people exploring further. If something is unknown I want to explore it because only when you know something can you decide whether you like it. My mantra has long been to get an *informed* opinion and then I make a judgement of my own. If more people did that, this world would be a happier place for a lot of people.

Like most of us who are considered *sensitive,* school was a nightmare of epic proportions because I never fitted in. Unless you were sporty or popular, pretty or a troublemaker there was a tendency you'd be overlooked. In the eyes of others, seeing what we call dead people, confirmed that the 'weird' category was made for me, and was entrenched further when it became known that when I skived off school I spent the time wandering around graveyards reading the tombstones instead of drinking alcohol, trying drugs or running with older boys. The teachers were used to dealing with those exploits. I was a whole new ball game and was the bane of their lives for not conforming in any way they knew how to deal with. So, like everything else people don't know how to deal with, they ignored my presence. I was delighted.

As my life unfolded I found myself in the midst of amazing experiences and although there are those who don't believe in life after death or choose not to believe, I have never been swayed from what I know to be true. And that's it you see—you must always go with what *feels* right for you. Not what organised religion feeds you, not what factions of society feed you—that is all conditioning usually borne of ignorance, control, power or just plain fear mongering. If others choose to believe in other things then great, each to their own and all that, but I *know,* borne of long and varied experience that physical death is not the end of our consciousness, not by a long chalk.

By way of introduction I would like to tell you a special story which explains why I have chosen the bee as my emblem. My great grandfather, Arthur Jeffery, was called up to the first world war when my grandmother was a baby. Before he left, an old lady gave him a small black cross she had made that had seven bees painted on it. She told him it would always keep him safe. He carried the cross in his breast pocket along with a photograph of his wife, my great grandmother, holding their baby daughter.

He was caught up in some of the fiercest battles and saw many of his comrades killed in front of him. In the midst of one such battle, while he was risking his life to save another man, he was wounded. He managed to get both himself and the other man, whom he carried on his back amidst a hail of angry gunfire, back to the trench. On examining himself, he found blood coming from his chest—a bullet that should have killed him had ricocheted off the cross. I still have the cherished photograph stained with his lifeblood. Thanks to that little cross he came home and lived a good life with people he loved.

As an interesting footnote to this story, when my grandmother died, my father found my great grandfather's medals but not the very special cross. He was gutted, to say the least, and assumed in my grandmother's failing health, she had probably given it away not remembering its provenance. He was telling me this one day and I suggested he 'asked for it back'. I explained that if something precious has been taken from us or we have lost it—by precious I mean of sentimental value not monetary—and we ask for it to be returned, it will turn up. My dad, lovely as he is and totally accepting of my abilities, was none the less, sceptical. But to give him his due, he asked aloud for the cross to come back to be in its rightful place with the medals. Two weeks later he rang me in a state of high excitement . . . he told me he'd had an overwhelming urge to get the medals out so delving in the depths of the wardrobe, having pulled out the suitcases and assorted detritus that was on top of the box the medals were in, he retrieved it. He opened the box and there laying on top of the medals was the little black cross with the seven bee's on it. He was as stunned as I was elated—magical.

St John of Chrysostom wrote 'The bee is more honoured than other animals, not because she labours, but because she labours for others'. This quote has huge significance for me in my life's work as a medium.

Now I don't pretend to have all the answers—anyone who does, in my opinion, is fooling themselves. We won't know all the reasons for our life experiences until we die ourselves but I know what I know, and all that I have experienced regarding contact with people who have died is good and true, and that is enough for me. I hope that as you read the following stories, the words of the people who chose to share their experiences with you bring you the insight and the comfort that was intended.

INTRODUCTION

"Can I tell you what it was like for me?" he asked.

I was sat there, in my lounge, reading a spiritual book about death—not that I'm a morbid sort, but I have always had an interest in life after death. I've experienced so much of it, it's hard not to. When I realised I'd read the same page twice without inwardly digesting a single word of it, I became aware that a male presence was trying to distract me. Knowing from experience that when a spirit person is trying to get through its pointless trying to ignore them, I said a hello and asked what he wanted. Immediately I felt my communication with him become as clear as if he were sat next to me. Which in a way, he was.

"What what was like?" I replied.

"My death." he said. "Can I tell you what my death was like for me?"

"Sure," I said, "hang on a minute while I find a pen and paper." Then I began to write everything, word for word, that was said to me.

Mark had taken advantage of the fact that I was quietly reading, to communicate with me. People in spirit form have a habit of doing this, as any medium worth their salt will tell you. People in spirit form have a habit of waiting until you have a quiet moment, then they're in like flint—often just as you are trying to doze off after a hard day or, as is frequently the case with me, when I'm cooking or reading. This is because in the doing of a simple task, you are operating on automatic pilot and your consciousness is easily influenced.

Mark told me that lots of others were waiting to tell me their stories too. I asked him what everyone wanted done with their stories.

"Use them," he said. "Use them to help remove the fear of death. So many people are living in fear of their own death, of what it will be like. Will it be painful? Is there really anything after death? We want to help them. We want to let them know that it's not the end, oh no, far from it," he said laughing, "far, far from it."

And he was right. So far to date over one hundred and fifty people from all walks of life have told me, in their own words, what their death was like for them. It was an honour that they should do so.

To maintain their authenticity and character I have written the monologues *exactly* as I heard them. Trying to replicate speech patterns was not always easy, but I hope that you are able to gain a flavour of their character with the reading of their story.

These are real people's stories, because that's what spirit people are—people. Not ghosts, nor entities nor any other names that the less well informed have given them in order to make it all sound spooky and frightening. They are people. People who have lived and loved like you do now, just no longer hampered by a physical body; that's all.

There are many books available on what people perceive death to be like, but most of them are written from the opinion of the author, and let's face it, we won't know for sure until we go ourselves. But this book—this book is a series of first-hand accounts from people who have made that journey, and want to give you the heads up, so think of it as a *Satnav For Your Soul*.

You can dip into it when you feel the need, or read from cover to cover. Some accounts are very funny because the people's personality come shining through—their love and compassion and sheer downright *caring* comes shining through. There will be stories that touch you deeply because they strike a chord with you. Take comfort from that, because that, my friend, is the whole reason behind writing it. In my experience, the people we love, who are just a little further along the path, are watching over us, cheering us on and loving us still . . . what could possibly be wrong about that? It's love. Love is the greatest driving force behind everything we do. It carries us forward and will, eventually, carry us home.

When I look back at the hundreds of experiences I have had, I realise how blessed I am and how *Satnav For Your Soul* is another step along that path. I hope you enjoy all the stories as much as I have enjoyed hearing them and writing them down for you. I hope that they, in some way play a small part in making your departure from this physical life a little less daunting.

If they do, then it has been an honour.

I will leave you now in the loving hands of the people who made all this possible. Of course, it is only right and proper to begin with Mark's story.

PART I
The Monologues

Chapter 1

Mark

The first person ever to come through to me; a remarkable young man who, despite or because of the hard, cruel life he had endured when he slipped through the cracks in society, chose to come through to bring hope to others. How sad that no one took the time to know his worth when he was here. And here is a lesson for all of us—never overlook that angry child, for he or she may be crying out for help or to be noticed, or the vagrant you pass every morning on your way to work. Try not to judge when you know nothing of what someone may have endured at the hands of others.

I was a bad devil, I was! Don't think I did a good thing for anyone in my life—even being born was a bad thing and I thought babies were supposed to be innocent—well not me apparently.

My mother told me I were a waste of space. Can you imagine that? A mother telling you that? Said she'd never wanted me and she only kept me for the benefits she got. Not that I ever saw much of those—there were no benefits living with her. All her money went on booze and fags. Used me as a fucking ashtray until I were nine, and the Social paid a visit. I had a t-shirt on that was too small. It rode up when I reached up to the door to let them out, so they saw the marks. Could have done join-the-dots on me they could—kept them busy for hours. Course, there was hell to pay then, finding the marks like that. I was taken away to the kids' home. Me mother were shouting about her benefits being cut now because of them interfering.

I can remember the smell of the social worker's car. Leather it was, the seats—brown leather. It was a bloke, the social worker. He had a woman with him who was really nice. He was a nice bloke too, but I could tell he was angry with me mother. He was doing his best to control it, but I knew: I know anger when I see it. Nearly had steam coming out of his ears he did. I was just glad someone had taken me away, even though it had taken nine years to do it.

The minute I got to the children's home it stopped being nice. Bloody cold there it was, and there was a right wanker in charge. Thought it was funny to belt the kids with a wet towel, those who weren't quick enough having a shower. Used to chase them, he did, flicking this bloody towel. Bastard. No one ever told on him, because we knew he'd get worse. He had absolute power, see—brutalised kids for years he did, until me and one or two others who shall not be named, scotched his little game. I'm not telling you what we did, but it weren't pleasant—that's all I'm saying, but he left us alone after that. Took us three years to get revenge, so he had a lot of payback coming his way.

I was a right little sod—weren't afraid of no one by then. I was never big for my age, but I was fast and wiry. Me and a couple of other lads used to do burglaries of a weekend when we were allowed out—sell the stuff to a couple of blokes on the local council estate and then hop it back to the home. No one was ever the wiser. How we never got caught I'll never know.

Then I got into drugs, didn't I! Did it for kicks first, and it was great. I was out of my head many a night. I fitted right in with the wrong crowd—felt right at the time. I was wanted, you know, not for my friendship I now realise, but because I was eager to please. I wanted to be liked, see—accepted, I suppose. Anyway, I fucked me head up good and proper. I'd left the home by then—well, kicked out really; "came of age" didn't I. Then it's, "Bye then. You can manage on your own now." Only; I didn't manage—not very well at all. I lived in a local squat for a while. Somebody's house, it was, not that I gave them any thought at the time. Trashed it we did. Not proud of that now, but at the time it was a good laugh. I spent years of my life nicking and doing drugs. What a fucking waste. Ended up in London. Went up west, where the money was. I begged, nicked—you name it, I did it. I even resorted to poncing a few times but it used to turn my stomach. I used to drink anything I could get my hands on. Regularly got a kicking from lads out on the town—skinheads mostly—proving how hard they were by kicking a drunk about. Clever.

I never mugged old ladies, though. Never mugged anyone, come to think of it. A Japanese tourist gave me his camera once. I think he thought I was going to rob him but I was just trying to get into the toilets as he was coming out. We sort of "clashed" in the doorway. I was dying for a slash and wasn't looking where I was going. I was out of my head, I suppose. All of a sudden he starts babbling away and thrusts his camera at me. I stood there, looking at this camera, put two and two together, and starts laughing. I also pissed down me leg, as I recall. Worth it though—I got twenty quid for the camera—probably worth £200. I never gave a thought to how frightened that chap must have been.

I know now how scared he was because I've felt it. Oh yeah; when you die it's not over, not by a long chalk. I've had to experience every bit of pain I ever caused anyone, caused them deliberate like. A real eye-opener it is, too. I also got to see why my life turned out to be a shit one, why my mother was the way she was. It was not pretty.

I took my own life when I was twenty-eight. At least I believe I was twenty-eight—I stopped counting birthdays. I was so wasted most of the time that I barely knew what year it was. I OD'd deliberate: couldn't stand it anymore. The money from the camera did it, that and a bit I had on me. Ironic, isn't it? That Jap chap probably thought I'd kill him, but his camera ended up killing me. Best choice I ever made. Believe it! Thing is—I'd never felt loved, see. Not in my whole, sorry, miserable, little life. So I thought, *"Fuck it. There has to be something better than this."* Stands to reason, doesn't it? I was already in hell, so heaven had to be out there somewhere.

I remember waking up in a bed and thinking I was in hospital. I thought, *"Fuck it, I failed."*

Then this bloke comes along, a doctor I think, and he says to me to lie still and sleep. But you know what, I heard him say it, but I swear his lips didn't move.

I thought then, *"Fuck me, Mark, you're still out of your head."* But I wasn't, see. Everything was clear, crystal clear.

Anyway, I nods off again and eventually woke up to find my old neighbour beside me bed, my neighbour from when I was little. Lovely woman; used to give me jam sandwiches through the letterbox when me mother had gone out. One time she took me in her flat and gave me Weetabix and hot chocolate until me mother found out and gave her a lecture and me a hiding. Didn't want to draw attention to us, I suppose.

I was pleased to see her, Mrs Collins. Nice old bird she was. She told me that I'd died. It clicked then. Mrs Collins was old when I was little, so she'd have to have been dead for years, and I mean *years*. Turns out she'd called the Social, and after about the hundredth time, they condescended to turn out. Me mother had guessed it was her and had gone for her with a whisky bottle when her benefit was cut. Mrs Collins had been okay but had a heart attack three weeks later.

I was pleased to be dead. It was the one thing I'd got right in all my life. Course, it took some getting used to, still being me but having no physical body and everything done by thought. But, best of all, I felt loved—loved by Mrs Collins and everyone I met. It was weird at first. I met relatives I never knew I had, all kinds of people. I was helped a lot; to understand my life—the way it was, the choices I made. No one was mad at me for ending it. I wasn't threatened with the fires of hell or anything like that. It's all rubbish, that is.

I'm happy now, really happy. I work with other young people with troubled lives like my own. I'm one of the welcoming committee, if you like. God knows they need a friendly face 'cause there won't have been many where they've come from. I'm not sorry I did it, not sorry I opted out. I'm just sorry I hurt people, people I'd robbed—I know now how it made them feel, and I'm sorry for that. But the rest—no, not sorry at all. I have a use here: I have a *life* here. Not a waste of space anymore. In fact, I don't take up any space at all. Just a pity I had to die to feel loved, really. Still, there's always next time. See you. Be lucky!

Chapter 2

FRANNIE

Frannie is a warm, lovely, gentle soul who came through to me on a cold winter morning as I was settling down to some ironing, a job that doesn't require all your thought processes to do. Frannie, sensing my reluctance to actually start the job, decided this was an ideal time to get my attention to tell me her story. She was right.

It was the long days, you know, long days that stretched into very short nights. I used to get up with Joe just after four in the morning, dragging my weary bones out of bed to make him a cuppa before he went to see to the cows. It wasn't so bad in the summer months, but the winter—oh, the winters were bitter. I've had to crack ice off my slippers more than once. Of course, if I hadn't worn them out in the yard the night before it would have helped. I was always doing that—I'd go to bed thinking all my chores were done and then I'd remember I'd left the washing out, so I'd get back out of bed and dash out to the yard in my slippers.

That's what happened that night—the worst night of my life it turned out to be. I had just settled into bed with Joe when I remembered I'd left the washing out.

"Leave it for the morning," Joe mumbled from somewhere underneath the covers; but I'm a tidy person see, I couldn't leave the washing out so out, I goes at the dead of night, in the rain. I could have left it out—my sister Ellen does that. She leaves her washing out for days . . . says she's letting it rinse through again. I said to Joe once "What if someone stole her underwear?" He said no-one would want it unless they were going camping because her knickers were the size of a two man tent.

It was very eerie outside that night. The moon had cast a silvery light across the yard and the old wall beyond—very pretty but a bit, you know, eerie. As a rule I'm not afraid of the dark, I was brought up in a house with no electricity, only candles we had, candles in jam jars. I could have done with a candle in that yard. I felt afraid, like someone was watching me, but I couldn't see a thing.

I went down over the grass to the washing line and began to gather it in as fast as I could. Pegs went flying everywhere—I wasn't going to bother about those. I was sure someone was out there, but the dogs were quiet, so I thought I must be scaring myself, and I told myself off for it, but I skipped and ran the last ten feet to the door.

I shot in the kitchen and bolted the door behind me; then I was afraid in my own kitchen, but I didn't know why. I'd never been afraid in my own kitchen before. I mean, it was my kitchen, where I had spent many a happy hour, or not, depending on whether Joe had tracked mud in for the umpteenth time. I threw the wet clothes on the table and high tailed it upstairs, I kicked my slippers off, then jumped into bed and tried to burrow under Joe to get warm. Only Joe wasn't as warm as he usually was, and he didn't complain when my icy feet touched his. He always complained about my feet, "Like blocks of flipping ice," he said they were, "blocks of flipping ice."

I said, "Joe? Joe love, are you alright?" He didn't answer me. I nudged his shoulder, like you do, not enough to wake him but just so he'd grunt to let me know he was still alive. Only he didn't grunt. He didn't do anything; he just lay there.

My heart was hammering so loud I couldn't tell if Joe's was still working or not. I didn't know what to do. I leaned over him to see if I could feel him breathing. I even got my old compact with the cracked mirror and held it to his mouth. Nothing. I sat on the bed and looked at him for what seemed ages but was probably only minutes. I was waiting for my brain to catch up and tell me what to do. Funny how your brain stops working when you've had a shock.

A fierce breeze whipped through the bedroom—it was always cold in the bedroom. Joe always liked a window wide open, summer or winter, and that night there was a force nine whistling through the room. I shut the window for the first time in forty years then I tucked the blankets up to his chin and kissed him on the nose just like I always did.

He had a very large nose did Joe: it took him years to grow into it! When I first knew him it seemed to take over his face but as he got older the rest of his face caught up with it and it suited him. He used to tease me.

"You know what a big nose means, don't you Frannie?" he'd say.

"What?" I used to say, all coy, like I hadn't heard the answer a hundred times before.

"Big hankies!" he'd say and wink at me.

Joe couldn't wink at me anymore. He couldn't track mud in anymore either—I missed that. I missed his nose pushing into my neck when we used to have a cuddle. I missed his big old hands on my waist waltzing me around the kitchen when a Glen Miller tune came on the radio. I missed the way his lovely blue eyes crinkled at the corners when he grinned. He used to look at me with so much love, even when we were knee deep in slurry or sheep dip. That's a test for any relationship, that is—if your man can still love you when you are splattered head to toe in slurry, then you have a good man. I missed him. I missed him every day in lots and lots and lots of ways but most of all I missed being loved.

I had to sell the farm. It was too much for me and I was broken hearted all over again. We'd worked hard all those years. I still woke at 4am for a long time. I often used to think that I must get Joe's tea, before I'd remember that Joe wasn't here to drink tea anymore; then I'd have a little cry, turn over and try to get back to sleep.

You must understand, my lovely, I didn't want to live anymore. Not without Joe, without everything that was familiar to me. I couldn't see the point. So on the day of the farm sale, when the last of the stock had gone, I sat in the yard and had a little chat with God.

I hoped he was listening because we had been strangers for a while. I told him I was ready to go—I told him I wanted to be with Joe, that I had done my stint here and when he had a minute would he collect me up. Well, he must have been listening because eight long months later I was taken poorly, very poorly—pneumonia, they said.

I was in the cottage hospital one night, just sleeping a bit, when I saw my Joe. I knew I wasn't dreaming. I really wasn't. He was stood there at the end of my bed.

I stared at him and said, "Joe? Is that you Joe?" He smiled at me and I heard his voice inside my head.

"Hello my darling girl," he said. He always called me his darling girl, even when I was long past being anyone's idea of a girl, he was funny like that.

"You coming with me?" he said.

I would have gone anywhere with my Joe, anywhere at all. He came over to the side of the bed and he took my hand, took my hand in his big warm farmers hand, and I slipped out of that tired old body just like you'd slip out of an old overcoat; and I was with my special man.

And that my friend is dying. No matter what you go through to get there, slipping off your old overcoat is so easy. There is nothing to be afraid of because the person you love most in the world still loves you—they will come for you and they will see you safely home.

Chapter 3

ROBERT

Robert died through a lack of love. "But don't make me sound miserable." he said. "There's nothing worse than a misery. I may not have had fuck all, but I weren't always miserable. Besides, I ain't alone now, so it's all good innit?"

'Ere, I tell you something—I didn't think it would be like it was, you know, dyin'. I thought maybe it would go dark, like, you know, someone flickin' a switch or summin'. But it weren't like that at all.

Flamin' light is what it was, whole flamin' room lit up, like Blackpool illuminations, it was. I fought (thought) "Old up a minute, what's 'appening 'ere then? I'm s'posed to be dead 'int I? This can't be right." I tell you, my brain was doin' somersaults. Light? Light when I was s'posed to be dead.

Course, it was confusin'. When I was a kid I was stuffed full of gory tales about the devil what comes to getcha after you die—if you've been a bad sod, that is. Well, I certainly ain't been no angel in me time—not *all* bad o' course—but not exactly all good either. So I was convinced that, after I died, I was more likely to be enterin' the fiery furnace than sittin' on a cloud. I was half expectin' that as soon as I copped it, the old devil himself would be puttin' in an appearance. Well, I got that much wrong, that's for damn sure.

I tell you what, you shouldn't 'ave no fear of death, certainly not in my experience. Now, I don't want to build your hopes up—I mean it ain't a bowl of cherries 'avin' to leave people that you loves, 'specially when they're all cryin' round your bed. But, blimey when you do, when you shuts your eyes for the last time, it's bloody glorious! *Glorious,* I tell you.

First thing I saw, just before I copped it, was me muvver stood there.

I thought, "Oh no, I'm for it now. What's she doin' 'ere?"

She was smilin' at me, all warm and tender and I just bloody melted. I mean, we weren't close you know, like muvvers and sons should be; I never did nothin' to make that 'appen—it just did. I didn't feel loved like the others, dunno why, I think that's what sent me off the rails a bit. I used to think; if no-one cares about me, why should I care about anyone else? It was an excuse to do bad things, stupid things. I brought trouble to the 'ouse, so stands to reason that she liked me even less for that. Our relationship went downhill and didn't stop.

I 'adn't seen 'er for years afore she died. Me sister told me, sent me a letter—I think I was banged up somewhere, so I couldn't 'ave gone to the funeral anyway. Not that there would've been much point, hell, me family wouldn't 'ave recognised me, I don't 'spect.

So, the years went on. I was in and out of nick more times 'an I can count: not a bright boy. 'Ad a couple o' relationships, 'ad a couple of kids through the years, never stayed wiv the muvvers. Good girls they were, but it was me—I didn't know how to carry on in a proper relationship. Flings, now I could cope with flings, but when they starts choosin' carpets and wall paper, I start thinkin' to meself, "Best get outa here boy."

So I buggered up most fings in me life. Trouble wiv me was I din't know a good thing when I 'ad it . . . dozy pillock. Anyhow, me life went from one mess to anuvver, one nick to anuvver, until I copped it, right there in the hospital—pneumonia, I'd heard. Not surprised! I'd been sleepin' out for bloody weeks; beginnin' to lose me 'ead a bit, an' all, I was.

Anyhow, as I said, I was in the 'ospital, breathin' me last, no cryin' relatives round my bed to hold me back from the brink. There was no-one at all wiv me when I copped it. I was just layin' there, breathin' through what felt like a wet rag when I thought to meself "I'm gonna die; I'll just shut me eyes for a minute."

And *then*, when I opened them again, or thought I did, there was me muvver stood by me bed.

I blinked, looked away, looked again, and there she was—I thought at first I was seein' things. I mean, I wanted to see her over the years. I missed her true enough, she was me muvver, after all. I'd always loved her, see, even when it wasn't returned. Couldn't 'elp it—I was her child. Natural, 'int it, to love your mum . . . even if she was a cow at times.

"Hello Rob," she says.

Well, I just bloody melted didn't I, I jus' bloody melted. She said it wiv such love, I couldn't bloody believe it. She'd never, not as I could recall, ever spoke to me like that—wiv love. You know, warm—surprisin' how much warmth you can put into, "Hello Rob."

"How come's you're ere?" I managed to say. Only I weren't speakin' out loud, it was like, in me 'ead, but as clear as anything.

She smiled at me and touched me hand. Hers was warm, warm I tells yer—I was confused. Me brain was tellin' me she was dead, yet I could see her clear as day in me room *and* she was warm, livin' and breathin' warm. I tell you I couldn't get me 'ead around it.

"You've died Rob," she says. "This is it, this is what it's like. I've come to take you safely home Rob, home where you should be."

I was just thinkin' to meself, "But why are you come, if you don't love me?" When it was like she heard me.

An' she says "I wanted to come Rob. I've been followin' yer life. I know I should've done a better job, been a better mother to you. I don't know why Rob. That's people innit? They's contrary.

I didn't know how to cope some days, so many of yer, and yer got lost somewhere along the line. I'm sorry Rob, I'm sorry I wasn't a better mother. I did love all of yer, I truly did, but I just didn't know how to cope. I was barely holdin' yer all together some days. I loved yer as much as I could, then I couldn't cope no more and yer runs off when yer was sixteen—never saw yer again.

I fought yer was dead for years then I'd hear yer'd been in prison again. I used to feel awful guilty sometimes but I couldn't say that. I 'ad to be strong for everyone else, holding them together. Yer lot was like a lot of loose ends, and I barely had hold of yer, but I loves yer all. Wasn't the best mother, I'll admit, and was overly fond of the juice, but, by Christ, it got me through many a rough day.

I wants to be friends Rob, I *wants* to be yer mother. Will yer come with me, will yer trust me to see yer safely over Rob? I wants to love yer, I wants to make amends, put the past right. When I came over, I got to see how yer'd felt as a nipper—I got to see where I went wrong Rob. Ashamed I am, ashamed and awful upset. That's why I'm here now Son, that's why I wanted to come get yer. I loves yer, I loves yer very much."

She holds her hand out, wantin' me to take it. I knew, I just knew, I would die if I did. So I reaches out to her in that darkened 'ospital room, and as our hands touched the room lit up like a belisha beacon—just for seconds—as I slipped right out of that knackered old body.

Soon as my hand touched muvver's I felt all the love flood into me, all the love she really felt. All the love I should've 'ad as a nipper, *wave* after *wave* after *wave* of it. It was worth dyin' to feel that. It was worth *everythin'* to feel that.

So you tell 'em—all the poor buggers out there that don't feel loved, what's been rejected and stuff—you tell 'em. "Make an effort with your life, you go ahead, and show the buggers you ain't giving in."

I shoulda done more with my life but I was young and stupid and nursing a grudge. It don't do you no good living like that, I know now. Stuff like this, shit in your life, is a kinda test, you know what I mean? I know what people say about love—how it's all rosy and stuff—well it is if you got some coming your way, but if you aven't, like me, like I was, you gotta think, "Sod 'em, I ain't wasting my life. I'll show you, you miserable fucking lot. I'll show you I can be somebody, I can make a difference in this world!"

'Cause you can, you know. You got all the tools inside you to do it. Don't let others be the excuse for being miserable. Otherwise they win, don't they; and you lose, you lose big time! So let my miserable fuckin' life be an example of how not to be, then I will know I done some good. That's all I want to say really—cheers then, cheers for that!

Chapter 4

Tony

Suicide is a highly emotive subject. Here Tony gives his reasons in an incredibly honest, open and succinct way in the hope that someone may just save their own life if they are willing to wake up.

Hello, I'm Tony. I hung myself in my garage. I just couldn't cope with life anymore. It was the gas bill that tipped me over the edge; that, and finding my wife in bed with my mate. I think that's enough to tip anyone over the edge. Obviously, finding my wife like that did the major damage, but you get the picture.

I knew we were getting divorced anyway, but you just hope, don't you—at least I did—that we'd work it out. But finding them like that just proved to me really that we had no choice. Well, at least I had no choice, she seemed happy enough.

By the time they got dressed and came looking for me I'd already done it—topped myself, kicked the bucket, done myself in. I'd read about people doing it in the past but I never realised how easy it was. I s'pose I wasn't thinking really, not clearly at any rate.

Only dying is not a bit like you think it will be, not a bit. You read that people have seen bright lights or heard someone calling their name, stuff like that— well it wasn't like that for me.

I wasn't scared, well not much. I didn't really know what was happening to me, so how can you be scared of something you don't know? That's like saying you're scared of flying, but you've never been in a plane—stupid.

I was alarmed enough to know I wasn't in my body. But I was in control of what I was feeling, and I was aware I was shaking, but that wasn't nerves, least I don't think it was. Everything was black, just black. Not a scary black, a soft velvety black; and I felt I was suspended somewhere in space, just for seconds, I wasn't hanging about in the ether for ages—that would be scary. No, I was just 'there', very aware that this wasn't what we call 'normal'. I certainly wasn't unconscious, because I could hear ok, so I figured I'd better just be still a minute, and try to get my bearings.

It was then that the blackness began to disintegrate . . . it got lighter and lighter grey, until I could make out the shapes of people—a bit like the film Ghost, remember that? The one where he dies, and he walks off into the mist and there are people coming towards him? Well it was like that. I knew I was straining my eyes to see who was there, but it was useless, they were just shapes; so I thought I'd just wait and see who turned up. To be honest I thought I was dreaming, but I knew I'd just hung myself.

One minute I was in the poxy garage, and the next I was surrounded by people. Sort of milling about waiting, they was, waiting for people who were dying. There wasn't anyone waiting for me, because they didn't know I was coming. I was feeling a bit lost, I mean, it was a bit strange—I knew I was dead but here I was in a whole other place.

Someone spoke to me, a man, and asked who I was.

I told him, and he said, "Ah yes, the suicide. Came in about an hour ago. Someone is on their way to meet you. You're a little early—about forty years to be exact." I felt like I'd been told off, but in a nice sort of way, if you know what I mean.

I asked who was coming and I heard a voice I hadn't heard since I was nine.

It was my granddad. He'd been hit by a car on his way to visit us, and had died in the road. I didn't get over it for donkey's years, well twenty years. I was thirty-nine when I bought the ticket—killed myself. God, I was so pleased to see him. Tell the truth, for a minute there, I forgot I was even dead. Weird, innit?

Grandad said we had to go—we were taking up room in arrivals!

"Gets like Piccadilly in here," he said, leading me away.

Grandad wanted to know why I'd come along so early. I explained and everything, but I could tell he was a bit disappointed. He said I'd have to see a review of my life: all the good and bad I'd done, see what I thought of it, see what I thought I'd learnt in my thirty-nine years. I wasn't keen.

It was a bit like watching a bad film—you watch it hoping it will get better, because you can't be bothered to get up and switch it off; only I couldn't switch this off. I saw what I did to my wife— the drinker I was. I mean, I knew I was, but I didn't think I was that bad, not at the time anyway. Drinkers always have an excuse for behaving like a dick! I just liked it, I liked being one of the boys, when I should have made time for her, my wife. I should have listened to her, instead of getting mad at her.

I felt ashamed when I saw that Christmas when I'd overdone it again, and belted her for mouthing off at me—alright I'd spent some of our Christmas money with the lads, but not all of it. I saw her sitting on the floor crying, and I felt her sadness like a knife wound, as some of her love for me died right there. That was painful.; I didn't realise. Christ, I was thick!

I saw loads more: I saw how my selfishness lost me a good woman—that's it you see, people need to realise they are responsible for what they choose to do to others. You can't expect to treat people like shit and they'll still be around. And you know what makes me feel worse? She forgave me. She sat one night holding my picture; talked to me she did, I heard her. I was in the lounge with her but she couldn't see me; she talked about our marriage, how she'd loved me, all the dreams we had. She asked why I had to drink so much.

I wanted to shout out, "Because I was a dick!" But I knew she couldn't hear me. I think she felt me though, she wrapped her arms around herself and began to cry. She was rocking backward and forwards on the sofa, crying.

"I forgive you though." she said, "Wherever you are, Tone, I forgive you, I hope you're ok!"

I was proper choked, proper choked.

I had to go then, I couldn't stand to see anymore. But you know what? The anger left me. It left me because it was never mine to own. I had no right to be mad with her for leaving me. I drove her away—me being a selfish dickhead drove her away. It was hard to swallow, that. It's human nature to be mad at other people for not getting our own way—I wanted to drink like a bloody fish and still have her run around after me, and that ain't right, that ain't right at all.

She lost herself in my drinking; she got quieter and quieter as she moved away from me, emotionally I mean. We still lived together, but I can see now that she was only there in body, because she thought she could help me. Trouble was, I didn't think I had a problem, so I didn't need any help—what a dick.

I hope people learn something from this—if one person wakes up then it's worth it—that will be one less dickhead in the world, eh?

Cheers then, and thanks for listening. Thanks . . . thanks a lot.

Chapter 5
Arthur

War has claimed the lives of so many people that sometimes their numbers are in danger of just being a statistic; when, in fact, each and every person whose life was taken so brutally was a living, breathing human being. Someone's much loved husband, father, brother or son. Each one grieved over, and terribly missed for years and years by parents, wives, children, siblings and friends.

Arthur was such a man, but he, in the face of his own death, and with supreme selflessness, thought only of making his passing easier for someone he loved, how many of us could do the same in his shoes?

I idolised my father all my life. Despite what had been, for him, a very hard life, he was a good and loving man. When he was dying, I asked him when I would know I was as good a man as he was. He gripped my hand, smiled at me and told me that when I was loved by a good woman, and when I could help my fellow man without a thought for myself, then I would be a man.

Years later, I had lost track of what day it was. I knew the month was July, and I was in France, not enjoying myself. It was hot and the smell of rotting flesh and death was everywhere. You could taste it in the air you breathed and the water you drank.

I was lying there, in a hospital tent, with a fingertip grip on my own sanity, as every fresh bout of shelling tipped some of the wounded down into unexplored levels of madness and screaming panic. Every now and then, a walking wounded would shake my hand and tell me I was for a medal, you're a hero they said. I didn't feel like a hero. I didn't want a medal. I just wanted to go home. We all did.

My chest looked and felt as though someone had stuck a firework into raw meat; and the fire in my lungs, courtesy of mustard gas, did nothing to improve my mood. I lay back in my cot and thought about the recent events that had landed me there: I had a pin sharp recollection of battle, noise, blood and the general carnage that shelling induces. I didn't need to revisit that part as it was going on all around me, in the distance, and up close in the minds of the sleeping men who surrounded me in that field hospital. I lay there and wondered about our officer, did he make it?

I called to a nurse, who was able to tell me that he had survived but was in a bad way. Both sad and relieved, I offered up a prayer for his survival, then my attention was caught by the moaning of the lad in the cot across from me.

He had lost his legs, and what was left of his life blood was soaking though the sheet and steadily dripping onto the grass. He didn't look any more than seventeen; laying there all pale and small and calling for his mother. A nurse shushed him gently, and gave me a look which said they couldn't do any more for him. He continued to cry for his mother throughout the night, then, around 3.30am, I woke to a strange feeling in the tent.

I propped myself up on my one good arm and looked around. Most men were sleeping peacefully, although here and there several were still fighting the enemy in their sleep, flailing non exist limbs as they fought for their lives, poor sods. The nurses quietly moved among them, administering medicine to the worst, and soothing words to the others.

I looked across at the boy, who was strangely silent, and momentarily wondered if he had died, but he was watching a woman walking down the tent toward us. My eyes had been affected by the gas, so I was lucky I could see anything at all.

As she got closer to us, the boy was instantly animated, and held out his arms; the woman moved smoothly to his cot and gathered him into an embrace that both fascinated me and embarrassed me. I felt I was intruding, but they were oblivious to everything around them. I looked away to see if anyone else could see them, and was about to ask the nurse who this woman was, but I realised she couldn't see her, only I could.

I realised in that instant that I was witnessing a man die in absolute peace—this was his mother. As God is my witness, that boy stood up on legs he didn't have anymore and walked, walked I tell you, out of that tent hand in hand with his mother. I lay back down and was filled with wonder for hours.

I woke to the sound of fresh shelling, and the screams of the newly wounded and battle scarred, and thought again of home. I longed for home. I longed to see everyone again, to walk the village streets again, my mother's fireplace, my feather bed that swallowed me up in its comforting warmth, my wife. Oh, how I longed for my wife. My lovely, lovely Jenny.

I reached under my pillow for the card she gave me the day before I left: it was now stained with my blood, but I could still read her words of love on the back. She would never know how much that card sustained me in my darkest hours. I had read those words a hundred times, and never had they meant so much to me as they did now. My wife was a wonderful woman and I had never been happier than when we were together, and I so wanted to live for her, but I knew I had witnessed something miraculous the night before and I wouldn't have seen that unless I was going to die too. I don't know how I knew that, I just did.

The remainder of my day was spent writing a long letter to my beautiful Jenny, telling her how very much I loved her and how sorry I was that I wouldn't be there to fulfil the future we had planned together. I wanted to free her so that some time in the future she could hopefully begin another life with someone who would love her as much as I did. I wept as I wrote, knowing how heartbroken she would be. I wept for the loss of our dreams, the loss of her and the life we would have had. My sleep later that night was filled with memories of her and the strength of her love for me.

I felt strangely buoyant the next day because of that, and even more so when I was told that our officer had turned the corner during the night and his recovery was more certain. Some official chap came to see me later that day, and asked me to relay to him what had happened out in the field.

The shelling had been pretty bad—all that noise, explosions lifting men right out of the earth, splitting our eardrums. The enemy had to be driven back at all costs—we were firing wildly at anything that moved, some of the men were so jumpy it's a wonder they didn't shoot each other.

We had to run across this piece of land, nothing more than a field it was, all churned up with mud and bodies. The noise and the smell was unbelievable, it was like running into hell.

I remember hearing the shout to retreat, and beginning to dodge back to the trench, someone grabbed at my leg—it was a mate. He couldn't see a damn thing, he was hit badly somewhere. I dragged him back to the trench and rolled him down into it. He was crying and moaning about the pain.

"Its alright!" I told him. "Medics are coming." They carted him off somewhere.

We had a count up in the trench—we had lost a lot of men, and could hear some of them shouting out there. That was bloody frustrating, hearing them shout like that, some of the shouts getting fainter and fainter—I couldn't bloody stand it.

Someone realised our officer was missing. He was a good man to us all, a fair man, he had looked out for us at every turn and in unimaginable situations. A good soldier, not like some of them, wet behind the ears and no idea how to lead men. Someone said they saw him fall early on in the battle. We were sad about that, but I just had a gut feeling he wasn't dead. Before I knew it, and against what should have been my better judgement, I began to scramble out of the trench. Some mates tried to pull me back.

"Don't be a bloody fool," they said. "You've been hit yourself." I looked down and saw blood from my chest to my waist: I didn't feel anything so guessed it was someone else's blood. I pulled myself out of the trench, and went back out there amid the hell of gunfire and bodies to find him.

How I ran, I don't know, how I was missed by a bullet, I don't know either, but something stronger than me was pulling me forward. I shouted and shouted for him and heard a noise to my left. I ran toward the sound and found him face down in the mud, with half of some poor bugger on top of him. I rolled the body off and half dragged, half carried our man back to the trench. My mates saw us coming and risked their lives to help us—we fell into the trench amid a hail of angry gunfire and that's all I remember, until I woke up in my hospital bed with my lungs on fire.

I had been hit after all: got shrapnel in my chest, and a bullet went clean through my thigh. Bastards.

"You're being recommended for a medal," the official said.

I lay back, tired out, and said that I'd settle for my life. He shook my one good hand and gave a sad kind of smile, before leaving and letting me settle back into the welcome embrace of sleep.

I woke again around 3am, the atmosphere in the tent was electric—all around me men were sleeping soundly—no shouting, no thrashing as there usually was. I looked around, the air felt expectant. That is the only way I could describe it—like something was waiting to happen.

My attention was caught by people entering the tent, they moved silently between the beds searching the faces of the sleeping men. I was transfixed as I watched men without limbs arise from their broken bodies to embrace the people who came for them: I saw excitement on their faces. I watched as they embraced and laughed and cried. There was so much love in that tent, so thick, that I felt I could reach out and touch it, so amazing to watch and so, so emotional to feel. I was again filled with wonderment and awe.

An elderly man was the last to come into the tent. As he walked toward me I gasped aloud, "Oh God! Oh God! Dad! Dad I'm here!"

As God is my witness, the man I had loved and admired so much in life was stood by my cot smiling proudly. He saluted me, held out his hand, and said, "Now you are a man, my son. Come on home."

Chapter 6

DANNY

Cancer claims a great many lives and is no arbitrator of class, age or gender, Danny accepted his fate with humour and a courage borne of his dreams.

Dying is quite a boring process really, especially when you have no control over it. I was stuck in a bed most of the time, doped up to the eyeballs on god knows what—whatever it was, it was effective 'cause I never had any pain. I heard that people with cancer suffer a lot. Remembering that frightened the shit out of me when the doc told me I had it, but thank Christ I never had the really painful kind. I didn't need drugs until I was near the end, and that was only because there was a problem with my bladder, an infection or something ghastly. Anyway, it was uncomfortable whatever it was, so they gave me stuff for it. I slept mostly—sleep was an escape from the situation I was in. Dreams can carry you far, far away from everyday troubles.

I saw a woman in my dreams—she was always on a hill waving to me. When the dreams started, she was always in the distance, and I couldn't make out who she was but I knew she was waving at me like she knew me so I would wave back. It was always sunny and warm, and I was always out walking—my favourite thing to do when my legs still worked, so to walk in my dreams was fantastic. I'd hear birds, I'd feel the grass beneath my feet, the wind in my hair—I was there. When I'd wake up I'd be annoyed and disappointed to find myself in that poxy bed, and very puzzled as to who the woman was.

I had no-one to ask, which was awkward, and any family photos were lost in a fire many years ago.

I began to look forward to my dreams. I even asked—mentally that is—I asked to see this woman a little closer, to see if I knew her, because she certainly seemed to know me, but she was always on the hill out of reach. I remember that the sun was always behind her, illuminating her silhouette, nice touch of the celestial, I thought. That's another thing—my sense of humour; but when nothing else is working for you, you gotta hold onto something.

I spoke to the doc about these dreams: he looked about nine years old, and clearly hadn't had enough life experience to understand where I was coming from. He was nice enough, but I switched off when he tried to explain how complicated the human brain is, and what drugs can make you see. I didn't need the scientific jargon—I just needed someone to tell me this could be real, because it most definitely felt real to me.

It was another two weeks before I dreamt of her again. This time she was closer—she waved and I waved back. I could clearly see her on the hill, I called to her to wait, but she just smiled at me and started walking away. I began to hurry after her—I was busting to know who she was, why did I keep seeing her? I couldn't catch up with her, she was always too far ahead of me and then just as I felt I was gaining on her, I would wake up, and that really pissed me off.

As my dying progressed, I dreamt of the woman again, but this time she waited for me to catch up. As I got closer, I could clearly see her features and her amazing chestnut hair. She seemed familiar, and I felt my heart constrict as a long buried memory flashed into my mind.

I am four years old and I can hear a terrible noise of distress coming from my mother's room. I wake instantly and run to her, but I cannot see for smoke—my mother is on the floor reaching for me. Our fingers touch briefly before someone snatches me from behind, and tears me away from her.

I am bundled outside by someone who is very strong and passed to neighbours, who hold me as I thrash and scream for my mother. I can see the house collapsing into the fire and all I can hear is my screaming.

In the dream the woman touches my arm and the memory instantly vanishes. I looked into her green eyes and she smiled at me—my heart constricts again, I know her! Oh God! Oh God! I thought, let this be true! *Please, please let this be true.*

She touched my face to get my full attention, and made the sign—our sign. I love you. I remembered it! After all these years, I remembered it! I frantically signed back to her; I love you, I love you! I was overjoyed, *absolutely overjoyed*.

She turned to walk away, now holding my hand, and I understood that I was allowed to go with her and my heart was *exploding* with happiness. My mother had been deaf and had taught me to sign from when I was so, so small but I had buried that memory, along with the intense trauma of her death, the pain of losing her and missing her terribly for forty nine years. And that, for me, was dying.

I will tell you something . . . if someone you love is very ill, or close to death, and they tell you they have been dreaming a lot of someone they love who has already passed, then believe them, because when their time comes, they will come for them and love them and keep them safe. If you cannot recall the face, the voice, the touch of someone you love when they have been gone from you for a very long time—don't worry. *When the time comes, you will see them, you will remember them and they will come.*

Chapter 7

Rosemarie

I was sat in the garden enjoying a morning coffee before the day got underway when Rosemarie entered my thoughts. I got up to get a pen and paper, as I always do, and as I took my seat again in the morning sun, I listened to this lady who spoke openly about her shortcomings. She was at times funny and insightful, her voice fluctuating between how she really spoke and the voice she had obviously cultivated to become the lady she thought 'Rosemarie' to be. We all have a 'telephone voice'—the one we use to call the bank, and then there is the voice we have to call the children in for tea. This was very obvious when listening to Rosemarie, and was in direct contrast to the squalid boarding house room she clairvoyantly showed me where she had spent her time between jobs.

I was a chorus girl. I did other jobs before that: shops, cleaning—not that I was any good at any of them. They were very short lived careers. They were just stepping stones to where I really wanted to be—on the stage. And I had what looked to be a glamorous life, well, for a while, but this was mostly on the outside. On the inside I was a mess; a drinker and a depressive—a lethal combination.

Sadly my looks left around the time my love did—walked out on me for a younger, prettier, sober, woman. Same old story, can't say I blamed him. Well I did at the time but now, now I can see what a self-destructive path I was on, but I will get to that bit in a while. Now that my head is clear, it has been clear for a very long time, but this is my first opportunity to come through to someone like yourself and, truth be known, I'm a little giddy with the excitement of it all and I am liable to wander off track as I recount things to you, but bear with me.

I left my life, my physical life—not that I knew there was any other kind of life, existence whatever you want to call it. I had no idea that my spirit was separate from my body; fascinating isn't it? Anyway I'm doing it again—I was always told off for that you know, going off at a tangent, but hey ho, that's me all over! Anyway, as I was saying, I made my less than graceful exit from the world with the help of cocaine and alcohol. It was quick, and let me tell you, it was the best thing I ever did. I had attempted it before, suicide, I'd attempted it several times, but in a half hearted way. I think I just wanted the mental pain to stop, that's all, just stop so I could enjoy my life all the time, not just when it was fuelled by cocaine.

Harry got me onto cocaine; he was a rake, he was, proper ladies man. But I fell in love, in love with a man who charmed me with his looks, his body and his white magic, as he called it. But I always needed more, I was like that, I'd find something I liked, that worked for me, made me sparkle, lifted my confidence and I would over do it, become dependent. Harry found me existing on baked beans— oh we had to be so *thin!* I existed on a tin of baked beans a week! Can you imagine? It was no wonder I got hooked on the white stuff—took away my hunger pangs and lifted me to giddy heights. Of course, there had to be a comedown, and boy, did I always come down with a bump. I suffered the blackest depressions; they ruled my life, they ruined my life, my confidence, my worth as a human being. People need to understand more about addiction—you can't fight it, it consumes you. Well it does if you have no will power; I must have been behind the door when they handed that out *(she laughs)*.

Of course, looking back, I was addicted to Harry too, but Harry had an addiction of his own, namely women and money—if you had a vagina and a job you were his prey. He had charm by the bucket load, did Harry! I met him backstage once, he was chatting to some of the girls then saw me or somebody who was behind me. We were in a tight space, so he put his hands on my waist to move past me—told you he was smooth—when he winked at me, I was hooked. I had seen him around for several weeks, lazing about back stage, making the girls laugh, looking good in his trilby, and knowing it. He was always occupied with someone or other, until I became his next target.

I like to think he loved me, but I don't think he did, not really. I had a wage packet and was just another vagina to be conquered, I think. Anyway, I'm doing it again, you don't want me to get started on the Harry thing, I'm liable to go on for ages! In a nutshell, our non exclusive relationship existed of sex, booze and coke. When I had no coke I was as miserable as sin, and sank into depressions so black that even Harry couldn't haul me out. He'd pawn something of mine, or told me he had, then he would reappear with his white magic and some loving, often smelling of some other girl, *ugh!* When I think of it now it makes me wince at how tawdry it all was, still, you don't see that at the time. I was convinced I was going to hit the big time and Harry would help me. When it all came crashing down, as these things do, I just couldn't cope, or didn't want to cope, or both; and that was it.

When I awoke in a hospital bed I thought I had failed again and was intensely miserable. I heard a man speaking to me, he was dressed in white, and began explaining to me that I was in a safe place now. I asked how long I had been there.

"Oh a while" he said. "You've been sleeping and receiving healing all that time."

"How?" I said, "I haven't had any medication, how can I be healed?"

He smiled and said, "We have no need for medication here." And he just looked at me in a knowing way, waiting for me to grasp the situation myself.

"Have I died?" I asked.

He replied that I had, and that my arrival had been anticipated for some time. I thought of my son and was deeply saddened, and felt terribly guilty. The doctor, as I assumed him to be, touched my arm and told me that my son was being well cared for, and although he would always miss me, he knew it could only ever have been this way.

I have to tell you that I am with him often—I have watched him grow and become successful. He suffers with depression too, although only those closest to him would know. He feels my presence; I try to guide him as best I can.

We cannot have a huge influence—there is such a thing as free will that cannot be interfered with unless you ask for it, but it is still possible to make a difference here and there. It is a truth that we walk among you daily; that idea you suddenly had, those words to a special song that you just heard or fell into your head as you thought of someone you loved—all evidence of our influence. Some of us have unfinished business—mine was to guide my son to the pinnacle of his career; I have done that from here.

So, if anyone is reading this who longs to be a dancer, I can help them with that. I can inspire people from here. I know all the tricks *(she laughs)*: how to hide your nipples, how to do high kicks without dislocating your hip (that was a killer!) I had to get my foot above my head, my leg in a straight line; by the time I had mastered this my legs could swivel in their sockets. All you have to do is ask me . . . just ask out loud or in your head for Rosemarie, that's my name, it was my stage name. I was really called Brenda, but, and no offence to all the Brendas out there, but it's not the name of a dancer is it? Not really. Brenda sounds like someone who would be stomping around the stage in hobnailed boots. I chose Rosemarie after my Aunt Rosemary. I dropped the Mary because it still didn't sound like a dancers name, didn't sound classy enough. As I said, I know all the tricks. I still move among dancers from time to time; the theatre ghost you hear about is often me, or others who still wish to 'feel' the old ways but don't want the angst that goes with it. I can guide young women through the pitfalls of a life like this, because I lived it, and everyone could do with some help. Just ask—I will reach you through your intuition. You will feel me, and one day, you may even see me backstage, silently cheering you on.

I have to wrap up now—I'm a little tired, this is hard work—so the finale to my story is, without the addiction to unsavoury men, alcohol and cocaine, I am free to be the person I so wanted to be. Some of us need to free ourselves. Please don't think badly of those who take their own lives; we are not punished, we are healed and we are loved and we are free, and some of us are busting to help you to get it right! So ask, what do you have to lose?

Cheerio darling, this has been exciting. Cheerio.

CHAPTER 8

SHARON

Sharon was a victim of child abuse. She shares her story because she cares about others. She said, "If my story helps one person to tell someone to get help, before they end up like I did, then it'll be worth it." I need add nothing else.

'Ere for fucks sake, what's all this about eh? I mean, I'm not sure I want to be talking to you like this. I mean, how can you understand my life? Christ, even I don't understand my life, an' *I fuckin' lived it*. Well, I don't know that I actually lived it—I sort of drifted through it on the back of alcohol an' drugs, but I was there.

I didn't always take drugs. I must 'ave been about eight when I had my first hit. Someone was babysitting or round my mam's for some reason—she was on the game then so it could 'ave been a punter, I dunno—anyway, they was definitely a wanker for givin' that stuff to me. It made me fuckin' cough an' cough for ages. I remember my head feelin' funny an' a bit swimmy. My Mam was laughin' an' so was the wanker. They made me finish this funny fag, and in the end I felt sick an' had to go to bed, well, what passed for my bed anyway—it was a pile of coats an' old blankets mostly. Mam had sold my bed ages ago to some friend of hers . . . she promised me a new one but even at eight years old I knew that was a lie.

When I was twelve, I was sent to one of Mam's friends for a while. I was a bit suss (suspicious) to begin with, 'cause Mam's friends were usually low-lifes, but this bloke was a cut above. I knew him, he'd been around us for years, so I had no reason not to trust him. He was always ok to me, but I didn't know what the fuck was goin' on—he said he was goin' to look after me 'cause Mam had to go somewhere. He took me to his house an' gave me loads of pop and stuff. We had roast chicken; *I loved it* but after that night, I never wanted to eat the fuckin' stuff again. I started to feel a bit funny after drinkin' the pop—I know now that it was full of pissin' vodka—I started to feel sick an' I just wanted to sleep. He put me on the sofa an' covered me up all cosy.

I must 'ave fallen asleep 'cause I woke up to feel his hand in my knickers. Dirty bastard. I was fuckin' scared an' tried to fight him off but it weren't no fuckin' use. He was a bloke an' I was a scrawny little kid. He told me that Mam had used me to pay her debts—she owed him for her drugs so I best shut the fuck up an' take it or she was in trouble. He kept me there for three days. Fuck knows how much she owed the bastard.

We had the Social round our house a few times, but they was thick as shit. Mam used to lie through her teeth, an' they bought it every fuckin' time, 'cause they wanted to, besides I always looked ok. *I was a fuckin' mess inside, but they never looked that far.* Eventually they stopped comin'; no-one was ever interested in my welfare—even my own fuckin' Mam wasn't interested. She spent most of her time out of her head. That started my downward slide into drink an' drugs.

All of it was escape really 'cause it was a fuckin' miserable life, it got better after I left home. It was a fuckin' relief not to 'ave Mam's punters tryin' to paw me all the bloody time. I left home when I was fifteen. I lived in a squat with some mates till we was chucked out, an' then we found another, an' another, an' another. We had some right laughs, but how funny any of it would be when we weren't out of our heads, would be another matter.

I tell you what—I was fuckin' determined not to go on the game, *an' I fuckin' didn't neither.*

I did shoplift though, *I was fuckin' ace at it.* Nearly got caught twice, but that was it. I was fuckin' fast—out of us, lot I was the best at thieving. I took orders, an' got loads of stuff for everyone; in one place I had a deal goin' with the *pissin' store detective!* She would turn a blind eye when I was in, as long as I nicked stuff she wanted too, laugh or what?

Anyway, like I said there were times when we had a laugh, but lots of times I was pissed off with my life. I mean it weren't nothing special, an' I couldn't see a future. I mean I loved the idea of havin' a nice house, an' a nice bloke, an' kids one day, but how realistic was that? All I could see was that I might end up like my Mam, but that scared the shit out of me; I was bloody well determined not to go that way.

I started using aerosols, 'cause others did an' said how great it was, how it made you feel out of it—apparently you saw lovely colours an stuff.

Well I was 'avin' a shit day this day, it was the day after my seventeenth birthday an' *no-one remembered it*. I told myself I didn't care but I did really, I was really pissed off about it. So when I saw the aerosol lying there I thought, "What the fuck, I'm going to try that."

I saw bright colours alright.

I saw every colour under the fuckin' sun, and felt fantastic! Everythin' went out of my head; everythin' that made my life shit just went away. Then everythin' went black. Not scary black, sort of soft, warm black, an' I felt as if someone was holdin' me—someone who cared about me—I felt that very fuckin' strongly. I wanted that feelin' to last. Then the colours came back, an' I felt like I was floatin' in colours, so *fuckin' beautiful it was.* An' love, *Christ, there was love everywhere. Everywhere!*

I knew something had happened to me. I knew what I was feelin', an' no-one else had ever described this to me. Then I heard a voice, not a loud voice, just a quiet gentle voice callin' my name. I didn't recognise it as someone I knew but (an' this is the weird bit) I knew somewhere inside me that this voice was someone who loved me, who knew me. You'd think I'd be scared fuckin' witless, but I wasn't. I was *fuckin' relieved*. I knew I was dead—no-one had to tell me, I just knew, *an' I wanted this lovely happy feeling to last an fuckin' last an' last.* An you know what? It has, it fuckin' has.

The voice? The voice was an Angel. An' you can think what you want to think about that, but it's true. That was what all the colour an' love was about. That's what *life* should be about really, innit? All colour and love, that's all anyone really needs.

If I'd had more of that, I would have lived longer, had a nice life like other people, but I didn't stand a chance really, not with a mother like mine. Still, she's got to answer for her choices, just like I had to see why mine were not so good. Not the dying bit—that was ace—no, the bits where my actions hurt people. The stealing and stuff—I'm not proud of that. I mean we all do stupid things sometimes, and I was doing it to get by, 'cause no-one was going to give me a job... not looking like I did and not 'avin' a proper address an' stuff, so my actions was for a reason. But you tell people—people like my Mam and her dodgy pal—they gotta see what they did wrong, how they cause others to have a shit life. They gotta sort themselves out, 'cause you can't hide nuthin' when you get here—that gives me some comfort I can tell you.

In the meantime... *I'm doin' absolutely great.*

Thanks for listening.

CHAPTER 9

IRIS

From a background cushioned by privilege, Iris volunteered for war duty and was forever changed. She shares her story in the hope that her experience, like water on arid ground, brings forth a new growth in enlightened thinking.

My name is Iris Cooper. I drove an ambulance during the war, I was a good driver. When I trained for the job—well you couldn't call it training exactly, we had to drive at speed around obstacles on a disused pig field, that was about the extent of it, but I was full of excitement and nerves and desperately wanting to do my bit for the war effort. Mother wasn't at all pleased, and threatened to disinherit me. Father, although terribly worried, knew I was his daughter through and through, and so would always do exactly as I pleased. Mother had plans for me which I was "selfishly mucking up," as the poor darling so eloquently put it, but I was not to be swayed.

So off I went, full of nervous anticipation and holding fast to Father's sage advice to "fuck up the jerries at every opportunity." I didn't know what opportunities would arise as an ambulance driver in which to apply his advice. He had never forgiven them for blowing his leg off the first time around, so this may have coloured his thinking a little!

My excitement at being an ambulance driver was short lived, when I began, with my colleagues, to pick up the badly injured young men. I hadn't seen many deaths before the war. My darling Grand-mama had died when I was little; and I once found our old gamekeeper half in and half out of a pheasant pen—he had keeled over with a heart attack and was a rather fetching shade of blue! I don't know who was more surprised: me, or the disgruntled pheasants still waiting to be fed. And my pets, of course, I had buried several of them over the years and was dreadfully upset each time—although Georgie, my favourite old pug, in his old age, had used the sitting room carpet as a toilet so many times that it never did seem to dry out. When he died Mother said, "Sod the war effort, we are having a new carpet. If I smell piss again it will be too soon!"

My career choice was certainly a baptism of fire, and I will never forget picking up my first injured soldier: the poor darling had terrible injuries, including the loss of both legs below the knee . . . such a fine looking boy too and he was so good when he was in such terrible pain. He held onto my hand as we put him in the ambulance, held on for grim death he did, and begged me not to leave him.

He told me his mother was called Marjorie, and to please tell her he had died a hero's death. Even in the face of his own death he wanted to make his dear mother proud. I held his gaze and kept telling him that I would find his mother and tell her what a fine son she had.

Then a curious thing happened, I've never forgotten it—he smiled. He suddenly smiled at someone only he could see and said just one word, "Pops". Just one word, "Pops" and that was it. Then the light faded in his eyes and he slipped away from us, away from fear and pain and noise, to somewhere I hoped was far nicer for him.

I was shaken to the core, but there was no time to dwell on anything or anyone; I dealt with so much death in so many forms that I gradually became numb to it. Not numb enough not to be compassionate, you understand, but if I'd let all the emotions on board I would have been a jibbering wreck, and no use to man nor beast. But I never forgot that young man.

Sometime later I tracked down and visited his mother Marjorie, she was a nice woman, although I could see that the death of her boy had aged her, and a deep sadness hung about her like a cloak. Marjorie lived in an old rectory, she had asked me in, and over tea I told her of her son's last moments on Earth. She was deeply touched to hear he had spoken of her. I told her he had died a hero's death—this was not a lie, because in my eyes every soldier who walked into a war, willingly or not, should be commended for doing so.

Marjorie placed a hand over mine and began to cry. After a minute or two she composed herself and told me that her darling son, her only child, made her proud just by being the sort of boy he was, and then she cried again.

Her pain was palpable, and in an effort to ease this somewhat, I found myself mentioning his smile when he died, and him saying the word, "Pops." She looked at me in wonder, and broke into a smile that so reminded me of her boy. She told me that Pops was *her* father, Dick's grandfather, and she had been praying to him daily to look after her boy, and to see him safely to heaven, if the war claimed him. Mrs Wallace told me, through her tears, that she could rest now, knowing that they were together.

I left the house profoundly moved by the whole experience; I had never really had a belief in the hereafter. Much as mother and the local vicar—whom my father believed to be on commission, such was his zeal—tried to rope me into church, I didn't have a religious belief of any kind. But this encounter with Private Wallace and his poor mother had changed something in me, and I can remember thinking to myself that I hoped someone I loved would come for me when I died.

A year, and many adventures later, I was visiting a friend's parents in the east end, and rushing across the road to an air raid shelter, when I saw my beloved Grand-mama across the street waving to me. I waved back, and in that split second I remembered that she had died three years before. As this thought registered, the entire street had a direct hit from a bomb, or something equally dreadful.

I remember nothing. Nothing except my lovely, lovely grand-mama hugging me. I knew I was not in a physical body anymore; I was shocked, angry, sad and happy all at the same time. I looked back at the devastation around me—the houses that were there before were now huge piles of rubble, people were screaming, and fires had started from ruptured gas pipes. It looked like a vision of hell!

I was full of questions . . . full of questions! My grand-mama looked solid to me, she *felt* solid, I was not hallucinating, I was dead . . . dead! And I could see my lovely grand-mama . . . I didn't know what to do with myself! This was so unexpected, yet so comforting.

My lovely grand-mama said, "Come along darling, there's nothing for you to do here." She took my hand and lead me away. Everywhere I looked people were meeting people, real solid-looking people, people they loved and hadn't seen for a long, long time. It was so wonderful, so calming, and then . . . then I saw darling Georgie running toward me, his stumpy tail wagging so hard that his entire back end had a life of its own. I scooped up my little dog and squeezed him to me, he was as deliriously happy to see me as I was to see him.

So my message to you, my reason for coming through is to tell you—to tell anyone who would listen, whether they believe or not—don't worry when your time comes. Whatever situation you are in at the time, wherever you are in the world, whether you are religious or not, don't worry. Because someone you truly love, and who truly loves you will have been watching over you, and will come for you. You will see them, I promise. Oh yes, and the much loved pets you had, you will see them too! They will be waiting for you. Love., that's what it's all about, just love.

Chapter 10

Harold

Harold, the archetypal grandfather, surveying his lot in life and considering his job here is done, was resigned to his passing but still longed for the mother he lost as a small boy

I had cancer; you know, the long drawn-out kind. One hell of a thing that was, more painful for the family than me. I'd had so many drugs I barely knew what day it was.

I had more grapes than your average vineyard. I couldn't eat them. The family were so sick to death of grapes by the time I left this mortal coil, they said they never wanted to see another.

They used to sit by my bed and talk to me. I heard them, heard every word, even the parts when they bickered about who was visiting tomorrow, and what time were the buses. They used to kiss me on the head when they were leaving, tell me they loved me, then off they'd go. I knew there were tears the other side of the door. They thought I wouldn't know; of course I knew—I could see in their faces that their emotions were hanging by a thread.

I was an old man, I wanted to go. I wanted to tell them that, not that I wanted to leave them, I loved them. But I knew if I could only leave that worthless body I'd be fine, be free. I knew there was something after death—had always believed it.

When I was a boy I saw my mother die. I saw her leave her body and go off with a man I didn't recognise. Later I found a photo of him in the bottom drawer of the sideboard. He was my mother's father. I knew then, I knew then with absolute certainty, that he had come to take her to heaven.

But I still missed her; I missed my mother all my life. Come the end, I lay in my hospital bed and asked her to come for me. I used to will her to appear. If it was at all possible, if what I saw all those years ago as a boy was true, I used to say to her there in my darkened room, if that was true then, please . . . come for me.

I knew the end was near when I saw a kind of white mist in the room. I don't know why that should alert me but it did. I just knew if I concentrated hard enough my mother would step through it. Of course, some would say it could have been the drugs making me see that, but one morning—a Thursday it was, at ten past nine in the morning—my mother stepped right into the room as large as life and twice as beautiful.

"Hello son," she said and held out her hand. I took it willingly. I felt six years old.

Chapter 11

Gwen

Gwen is a funny, self deprecating lady who was able to joke about her thighs while telling me her story, which only goes to prove that even in the light of their death some women still worry about their weight. Gwen was remarkable in that she fully accepted that her passing from this life has saved the lives of many others. How many of us could willingly go into a situation that scares us most, knowing we may never come out, and yet go anyway?

I drowned. Funny thing was, I hated water. Always did. I mean I'd have a bath like everyone else, but I wouldn't get on the water in a boat or anything, not even in a rowboat at the park. I don't know why I was afraid of water really, it was probably the fault of the swimming lessons I endured with a teacher who thought ducking his pupils under the water was 'character building'. My mother made me attend, I dreaded the lessons but Mother said all the best children went to this instructor so I had to go. Looking back, he was only the best at being sadistic, but I digress.

I had gone to the beach, on this particular day with the family and some neighbours' children; it was a smashing day, very hot. We took lashings of food, and lemonade, and I remember telling the children not to swim on a full stomach; I'd heard somewhere that it wasn't a good idea.

I lay down to read my magazine, and the others had gone off up the beach to watch Punch 'n' Judy. Alex, our neighbour's boy, he was twelve, said he'd stay with me. He was building a sandcastle with a gully to the sea, a beauty it was.

Next thing I know I must have dozed off, because when I woke with a start, Alex had gone. I sat up and looked around—couldn't see him. I got up, and shading my eyes, I looked up the beach, calling his name, nothing. Then I began to get this funny feeling in my stomach, panic really. I waded out into the sea to my knees. Then I saw an arm go up in the air, then it disappeared.

I knew, I just knew, it was Alex—don't ask me how. I couldn't see the person's head, but I just knew it was him. I turned and shouted up the beach for someone to help me. No-one seemed to hear me, it was so noisy. I knew there was nothing else for it, I'd have to go in myself. I couldn't swim very well at all, but you don't think of that at the time. All I knew was that boy was drowning.

I just threw myself into the water. I went under, then to my surprise, I came up again. The swimming lessons my mother forced me into when I was eight came to the fore. I thrashed about in Alex's general direction, praying the whole time. "Help me get to him," I kept saying.

Well, I did get to him. He held on to me for dear life. We both went under several times. I was so, so frightened but I couldn't show Alex that. I told him to kick his legs for all he was worth, and he did you know.

Then I felt someone grab me, someone very strong. It was a man who'd heard me on the beach. He must have seen us in trouble and had swum out. I was so pleased, so grateful. I didn't know how I'd have the strength to get Alex to shore. I was calm too, scared but calm. Funny, really, when I was actually in a situation I was most afraid of. I shouted to the man to take Alex, told him that I'd be fine (when really I was anything but). Alex got onto his back, and that's the last I remember really, them heading for the shore.

I tried to swim, but I had no energy left. I was so tired, so tired. I just sank. I didn't have an ounce of strength in me to kick anymore. I just went under. I don't remember taking in the water. I don't remember feeling anything except warm, really warm.

When I woke up, I thought I'd made it back and I was in hospital. Well, I was in a hospital of sorts. I wasn't surprised that I'd died, disappointed at first, but not surprised. I knew when I entered that water that I wouldn't come out alive. It was a decision I made, and I don't regret it, not for a minute.

Alex lived. I got to see what happened afterwards, like watching a re-run of a film. The man got Alex to the shore and raised the alarm—there was pandemonium. Then he jumped back into the sea for me, because he realised I hadn't followed him in.

I was floating when he found me—not a pretty sight. I never did like that bathing costume, it wasn't what you'd call flattering. It had one of those annoying frilly skirts that were supposed to hide your thighs—to be honest I needed nothing short of a marquee for that! My thighs were never my best feature, "Good child bearing hips!" my mother had told me I had. I think she was trying to be kind. I did point out at the time that my hips could carry half the African nation, but she wasn't amused and said something about it being genetic. I dropped the subject after that and reasoned that she wasn't all that happy about hers either. The man, he pulled me to the shore, I bet that was a feat in itself. And I was whisked off in an ambulance.

The family went to pieces for a while but they recovered eventually and remember me with fondness, I'm grateful for that. If I'm honest I still get a glow of satisfaction when I hear them recounting my tale of daring.

Alex . . . well Alex went on to have a good life. He became a lifeguard and lived in Australia for the rest of his life. He saved many lives over the years. I don't know if he would have taken that career if he hadn't nearly drowned. He named his boat after me, you know. I thought that was a lovely gesture.

I didn't have a very long life, or even a very interesting one, but my life and my leaving saved many others, so I think that's a fair price to pay. And that's the key, you see, that's the key to being at peace with yourself. "Did you do your best?" you'll be asked. "Did you care, really care for another human being without putting yourself first?" I got a big fat tick in that column, I can tell you, and I am very happy about that. Very happy indeed.

Thank you for listening to the prattling of an old lady, I don't talk about my exploits to everyone here. Besides, everyone's heard it before; not that I boast you understand, no, my task is to try to settle those who have given their life for another, we swap tales. And you know what? None of them ever regret it, not one. It's terribly gratifying you know, it's like belonging to a special club. Mother, with her grandiose ideas of status, would be proud.

Chapter 12

Alma

Alma came through to me late one evening as I was preparing to stop work for the night. She began, very tentatively at first, to tell me her story; it became obvious to me that I was interacting with someone who was as shy in death as she had been in life. And although Alma didn't express it, I was of the opinion that the lack of love from her mother had shaped her into this person, who was almost apologetic for being in the way. I was delighted to listen and to write her story, if it wasn't for grandparents the world over, some children would never know security and real love.

I always believed in spirits, even as a child. I sometimes saw them, and once, I tried to tell my mother. She said the only spirits that existed came from a bottle; even as a child I knew she was wrong, and I also knew not to mention it again.

Mum and I were not close; in fact we were poles apart, which is how she preferred it. I was a nuisance, I made a mess, I was too noisy; in fact I was too much of everything for my mother. So sad when I look back now, but then, then I just got on with keeping out of her way, and spent as much time as I could with my grandmother.

I loved my grandmother dearly and I loved her house. It was small and cosy, with rooms stuffed with treasures from the past. Granddad's bits and pieces were everywhere just as they were before he died, (I missed him as much as she did) and Gran said she liked it that way, because even though he'd driven her mad at times, she had loved him, and couldn't part with anything. My mother said it was morbid, but Gran used to say she would think like that, but there was nothing neat and orderly about emotions, and you couldn't just switch them off.

"Come to think of it," she said, "there's nothing neat and orderly about life, which is why your mother has spent most of hers like a coiled spring!"

Whenever I stepped into gran's house I felt loved. Not like our house, my mother was obsessed with cleanliness. She even vacuumed the curtains, and each pleat had to be exactly one inch apart. I always felt tense at home, as though I could barely breathe; that's why I spent so much time at Gran's.

I was visiting Gran one afternoon when she mentioned going to church—she thought she'd visit them all, sort of try them on for size. In the end she hadn't liked any of them. She said the buildings were nice enough she just couldn't get on with some of the people running them, and besides, she didn't want some impersonal devil dodger hammering the bible into her; so on the advice of a neighbour she was trying a new spiritualist church next. I decided to go with her. She looked round and said there were one or two that looked a bit odd, but overall, they seemed a friendly bunch and she even had a message. The last one of the evening the medium said was Gran's husband.

"Typical," said Gran. "Late as usual! He was a train driver in his day you know, he was always late then as well. It would appear some habits die hard." The congregation laughed, and the medium told her he was watching over her. Gran was pleased with the message, and the medium finished off the evening with a little talk about how our loved ones come to get us when we die, and how we shouldn't be afraid. Gran said she wasn't afraid to die, she was just afraid Granddad would be late.

She said, "I can see me sat there in the great waiting room in the sky like an orphan of the storm. By the time your granddad turns up, your mother will have arrived and started washing everything in sight. The Angels will be starched to within an inch of their lives, and God help any of them trailing clouds of glory . . . your mother will have the hoover out!"

Gran continued to visit the spiritualist church for another two years—she made many friends and there was a peace about her. She still missed Granddad but was settled inside herself, knowing they would be together again one day, as long as he remembered what day. During those years many of Gran's friends and acquaintances died. Gran said they were forming a human chain to yank her up when it was her turn, so she wouldn't be left behind.

I found her, one evening when I called in after work. She had died in her armchair beside the fire, a whisky on the side table, and a big surprised smile on her face. I guess Granddad out did himself and arrived on time. I took huge comfort from this, it sustained me in some of the darkest times of my life.

When I became ill, I would lay there in my hospital bed and think of them both, of how they had enriched my childhood by just being there, by just being there and loving me. Gran didn't give a fig for other people's opinions. She gave up trying to please my mother, her daughter, years before, because she knew my mother looked down on her in some way. It hurt her, I know it did, but she hid it well. I began to see my Gran regularly—there in the hospital, in my sleepy, just before properly waking state. I began to see her sat on my bed. Not every day, you understand, but I would have liked it to have been. I mean, I didn't know then just how much energy it took for them to actually turn up in person like that. I do now, now I know it takes a tremendous amount.

I began to smell whisky first, that used to make me smile—she loved her whisky and the smell took me right back into her arms as a child. Then she was just there one morning, before the nurses did their rounds. She was there on my bed, slightly hazy at first, but then she got the hang of it, and was clearer. This marvellous old lady, in her familiar wrap-around flowered apron of my childhood, was there as clear as day; then she spoke to me. I was startled at first because

I knew if I was seeing her I was going to die but the feeling passed and then I was peaceful, so peaceful.

"Yes, that's right dear," she said, "I'm a little early, but that's me all over. Your granddad will be along in a little while. I'm just popping in to say hello, to let you know we are close by." I gained tremendous strength from seeing her.

"It's all true, you know," she said. "It's all true what they say you know, there's no need to be afraid. When your old granddad gets here we shall be off, nothing at all to worry about." Funnily enough, I wasn't in the least scared. I'd had enough of my body letting me down, nothing worked anymore, and I was so tired, so, so, tired.

I came to one morning early, it must have been early because it was dark outside, that dark grey—you know how the sky is just before dawn, dark grey with streaks of light coming through—well it was like that. My room had a glow from the machines, I was comfortable, just watching the dawn struggling to make an appearance, when my grandmother started to form again on the end of my bed. This time she wasn't alone, my dear old granddad was with her—still in his old railway overalls just as I remembered him, smelling of engine oil and brylcreme. He winked at me as he hooked an arm around my grandmother.

She smiled up at him and said, "I think it's time Ted!"

They came to the sides of my bed, Gran taking one hand and Granddad the other, and I felt the strength in their hands. And the love, oh I can't begin to tell you of the love I felt go through me, right from my toes to the top of my head. I was loved right out of my body, right out of that tired, worn out, no good body of mine, straight into the arms of the two people who had loved me most in the world.

I just wanted to share my story because some people have parents who don't love them, but if they're lucky they have someone else who loves them more, and they must take heart from this. Concentrate your energies in life on the people who do love you—don't waste time on those that don't. I can see now that my mother was the blueprint, as you call it, for how not to be; and my wonderfully marvellous grandparents were the blueprint for just how to be—loving. That's all that matters in life and in death: how much you love.

Thank you for listening to my story, I hope it has been interesting for you. It is tiring coming through like this but I was determined. We should all be determined in one very important thing—how to love. That is what I believe, be determined to love well and then, in time, all will be well.

When it counts, all will be very well indeed.

CHAPTER 13

BILLY BOY

Billy Boy's personality came bowling into the room—very loud, very funny! He was as amused by his friends in his story as I was listening to him recounting it. He took his own life, but didn't want to be classed as a suicide victim—he stressed that he wasn't a victim of anything but his own selfishness.

I died in my car. I killed myself; mostly because I was fucked up in the head, had been for years. I couldn't keep a relationship going—I'd end up losing my rag and giving them a belt. Used to lose my rag on a regular basis, even worse when I'd had a drink. I loved them though, the women in my life, I loved them all, in my way. Didn't always suit them though 'cause I was dead selfish—did what I wanted to do when I wanted to do it. I couldn't stand it if they left me; I had to be the one doing the leaving, pride see—lot of fuckin' use that is.

I was given pills to take, because of my head being fucked up, anti-depressants or something. Didn't mix well with drink though, I used to dabble in the other stuff occasionally too, that didn't do no good either. I was a bit of a bad lad all round really—bit of crime here and there, receiving mostly. Got caught once or twice over the years and ended up with fines—more debt to deal with.

I just woke up one morning all depressed, and thought, "Sod it, I'm getting out of here." Nothing anyone said would have changed my mind; I was that sure it was the right thing to do. So I takes the hose off the vacuum cleaner, gets some tape, and off I goes. I parked where I knew I wouldn't be found until it was over, stuck the hose on the exhaust and through the boot into the back of the car, sat down to write a couple of 'sorry' letters, done that then dozed off. Simple as that. I didn't choke or nothin'—just felt myself getting sleepy and dozed off. Best thing I ever did. It was the right thing to do for me.

I woke up to find two of my old mates in the car. Matt was in front, and Ted in the back—they'd died in an accident years before. I'd always missed them, and now there they were. I looked at them, stared at them really, and heard myself say, "What the fuck?"

"Alright mate?" they said, grinning at me.

"Fuckin' great," I thought, "I'm hallucinating now."

"No, you topped yourself, you plonker. We been taking bets," Matt said. "Ted here said you'd make it 'til Tuesday. I said na—his latest bird has seen sense at last, look at the state of him, he'll be here sooner than Tuesday. And here you are now, come on, stop fucking about."

"Fuck off." I said, "You mean I'm dead"?

They looked at me like I'd lost my mind, which—come to think of it—in a way, I had.

"Course you're dead" said Matt looking at me like I was mental "We ain't come all this way for nothin'!"

Ted leaned over and said, "Told you he'd be hard work, that's another fiver you owe me."

Matt said it didn't count, 'cause we ain't got money where we are—it's a metaphorical bet.

"Meta-fuckin-forical or not, a bet's a bet!" Ted replied going into one of his sulks. I tell you, it was like old times. I sat there and looked at them, it all felt real enough to me.

So I said, "Right . . . if you're real, and judging by how you're falling out as usual, you are, so what now? What the fuck happens now? I ain't got to see God have I?"

Ted burst out laughing, punched the air and said "And that's another fiver! Told you he'd ask about God didn't I! That's his Auntie Jean for ya."

My Auntie Jean dragged me up, and I mean dragged me up. She got given me when I was a nipper and wasn't grateful for it. Saw it as her Christian duty to bring me up, she did—biggest bloody martyr that ever walked, my Auntie Jean. Real bible thumper, or to be more accurate, she thumped me with it, while reciting it chapter and fuckin' verse.

Matt looked at me and said, "No, you don't have to stand in front of God or nothing, it don't work like that, and before you ask—no, we 'aven't seen your Auntie Jean.

"Thank fuck for that" I said, "Ok lets go then." And that was it!

I don't remember leaving the car, I don't remember even moving. I think it's a mind thing, as soon as you agree to go, ('cause you're with someone you knows and loves so why wouldn't you?), soon as you agree, off you goes—easy!

'Course, there was a real sticky patch, where I got to see what I'd done, and the effect it had on others. I also got to see what my life would have become if I'd stayed, and let me tell you, I was fuckin' glad I'd left early.

You tell anybody out there that there ain't no punishment in killing yourself. That's what free-will is all about. If anything, you punish yourself by seeing and feeling everyone else's hurt . . . the hurt caused by you. It takes a *long* time to deal with that, not that there was much in my case. But you tell them that God, or whatever you wants to call him, (so many different names, bloody confusin',) well, him . . . God, he loves everyone. Even the fucked-up ones.

Chapter 14

Ethan

Ethan is a lovely, very naive, young boy who came through to share his experience of being bullied to death. In his words, he said he was fed up of it seeing it happen all the time, and it wasn't right that people died from being bullied. He wanted to let mums and dads and families know that when someone has died because of someone else, that horrible person doesn't get away with it.

"'Cause that's what they really need to know, it's only human!" Granddad says. They need to know the bully will pay for it one day, and like Granddad says, it doesn't hurt for the bully to know they can't escape. "Rats in a trap!" That's what Granddad says they'll be, rats in a trap, (I think he's still a bit annoyed!)

I was eleven, I didn't know nothin' really, I mean I wasn't a worldly wise kid like some. My mum sheltered me too much in some ways—if I had been a bit sharper I might have been able to get myself out of a scrape like I was in, but I doubt it. I mean, I didn't really know what was 'appenin' to me. I believed everybody, I did, how stupid is that? I 'ave to tell you though . . . I don't hold no grudges. I mean my mum didn't know—she thought she was doin' what was right for me—all mums do that, don't they? My mum weren't no different.

I loved my mum, she was great! We did all kinds of stuff together—she showed me how to make bread an butter pudding—I weren't all that good at it. One time I put too much milk in so it was a bit soggy, but my Uncle Pete, who was there, said he liked it that way 'cause it was easier to eat with his false teeth! They didn't fit proper any more, an' he could suck it out of the dish. My mum said he was disgustin', then she laughed an' hit him on the shoulder which made him choke, an' he spat his teeth into his dish, then we all laughed like mad for ages. Every time we thought about it for the rest of the day we laughed about it. That was the last time I made bread an butter pudding, I was dead soon after that. Dead as a blinkin' doornail.

I didn't know where I was or what had 'appened at first, and I missed my mum like mad—I mean *really* missed her. It was an ache in my insides—a really bad ache that didn't go away for ages an' ages an' ages.

When I was alive, if I didn't like where I was or what was 'appenin', I'd just shut my eyes, so now I was dead I did the same thing. I thought if I shut my eyes an' opened them in a bit, everything would be like normal, only it wasn't. To tell the truth, I thought maybe I was dreamin' or something . . . I mean it felt like that, a bit dreamy, but I *felt* a long way from home.

When I opened my eyes again my granddad was just stood there smiling at me—tell the truth that scared me just a bit—I mean I *knew* my granddad was dead. I even went to his funeral, so I knew for *sure* he was dead. I opened one eye an' peeped out, he was still there. He winked at me just like he used to, an' I went all warm inside. He could do that to me easy my granddad, he always used to wink at me, that was our special message, our special *I love you*. When he did it to me, my insides would go all warm like melted chocolate.

In a little quiet voice, I said, "Granddad, is that really you?"

"It surely is my boy." He said, an' you know what? *It sounded just like him.* I knew then that this really *was* my granddad, an' if I was dreamin' I was very 'appy about it.

"Where am I, Granddad?" I said.

"You are in heaven, lovely boy," he said. "You are in heaven with your old granddad, who loves you very much and is very glad to see you."

"In heaven?" I said, "In heaven? How did I get to be in heaven?"

Granddad took hold of my hand—I could really feel him holding my hand, he was warm and everything.

He said, "Do you remember the big boys?" I felt my tummy turn over at the mention of them—they scared me—I always had trouble with the big boys if I went out.

One time I was on the swings near my house with my friend Tim. We was only allowed to go to the swings 'cause we was together, but some big boys came an' started pickin' on us. We tried to run away, but they was bigger than us, an' faster. Tim got as far as the fence 'cause he was a faster runner than me, he got away but the big boys got me.

They weren't very nice people. They did some things to me that I never told nobody . . . *not nobody*. I had to run home without my trousers, luckily my mum was at my Aunty Jessie's next door, so she never saw. I put more trousers on, an' a few days later when she asked where my trousers was, I helped her search the house for them. She said they must 'ave bin stolen off the line—we often had clothes nicked off our line. Mum used to say that if stuff wasn't nailed down, any thieving 'whatsit' will 'ave it away. I didn't go to the swings again. When Tim came round he asked me what 'appened, an' I said they just roughed me up a bit then let me go, which was partly true.

Granddad squeezed my hand and said I had to try to be brave, 'cause he was goin' to 'ave to explain a few things to me. He said did I remember the big boys had chased me after I'd been to the paper shop?

I hadn't been out for weeks, an' my Uncle Pete had asked me to go to the paper shop. I didn't want to go—it was only at the corner of our street, but I didn't want to go. Mum said I didn't ave to, but Uncle Pete said she shouldn't molly coddle me so much, an' how I was big enough to go the shops.

"It's only for a paper an' a Mars bar, for heavens sake!" he said. "A paper for me an' a Mars bar for the lad."

Mum said I could go. I said I didn't want a Mars bar.

Uncle Pete said, "Well get one anyway you might want it later, get me the Daily Mirror."

I ran to the shop. I got the paper and a Mars bar right quick, an' when I came outside, they where there. I remember my tummy fell into my shoes an' made me feel *so sick*. I tried to go back into the shop but they wouldn't let me. They said how they was sorry for being horrible to me, how they wanted to be friends and said they wanted me in their gang and what I'd been through was something they'd all had to do to be in the gang. This is where I needed to be sharper, 'cause I would 'ave known they was lying to me. I believed them see, *wanted to believe them*, I was fed up of being scared all the time.

We went down by the canal. They said their den was down there, an' I should see it 'cause now I was one of them an' I could go there all the time an' 'ave great fun. I was scared inside, an' a small voice in my tummy was telling me to go home. I tried to look back up my road, hoping my mum was at the gate, but she wasn't. The big boys were all around me, I couldn't get away if I tried. When we got to the canal they showed me their den an' it was a good den. They had loads of stuff in it—they had rude magazines and a knife. They cut my Mars bar into slices 'cause gang members had to share everything. I didn't mind, I hadn't wanted a Mars bar anyway.

I don't want to talk about what happened in the den. Eventually when I thought it couldn't get any worse, I managed to get away, or they let me get away . . . then they chased me. They chased me right into the canal . . . I couldn't swim. I couldn't swim 'cause Mum couldn't, an' there was no one else to learn me. I died 'cause of the Daily Mirror an' a Mars bar.

Granddad said I was safe now; I *felt* safe with Granddad. He held me tight and told me that I would stay with him *always*. That made me feel mighty safe, I can tell you, mighty safe.

Like I said, I missed my mum loads. So bad, I thought I'd never get over it but Granddad showed me how to see her, and once I got the hang of it I visited her all the time. She *felt* me most of the time, I know she did, an' I used to hear her talk to me *all* the time, and she used to kiss my photo loads. Trouble is, it's very hard to make people like you—people what's still alive—feel us. Granddad explained how it's like trying to hear and see through a thick fog. We know we're heading in the right direction so we just keep goin', keep tryin' for all we're worth, an' eventually we get through. And then, you think it's your imagination or coincidence or because you're willing yourself to feel something! *That's so frustratin' for us!* Granddad says some spirit people give up trying to get through to people, 'cause no matter what they do, no one is satisfied or believes it's them. How frustratin' must that be?

I've been here ages now, ages an ages, Mum came to join us a while ago. She got cancer; Granddad said it was stress that did it. Mam said she didn't care what did it, she was just glad to be with us, she'd missed us for ages and dying couldn't 'ave come soon enough for her.

The big boys have grown up, an' have never told *anyone* what they did. Granddad said it didn't matter 'cause God knows what they did, an' He didn't miss anything . . . *absolutely nothing gets past Him*'. Granddad said they can't escape, and should they even try to slip through unnoticed when they get here, he's going to personally make sure he's on the gate with a reception committee.

Chapter 15

Brenda

It was once said to me that life is a rollercoaster, and there is no greater, more frightening rollercoaster ride than grief. There are points along the ride when you feel you are being pitched downward, into screaming madness and terrible unrelenting pain, then a little way along, you emerge briefly into the light, only to be pitched downward again, ambushed even, by a song, a half remembered story, a smile, a kindness.

Grief is indeed a journey, one that most of us have already experienced, and will, before the end of our lives, undertake many more times. Brenda experienced the myriad of tumultuous emotions and wishes to share with you the end of the ride, in the hope that when you find yourself aboard that rollercoaster you will remember her story and draw from it the comfort that she intended.

I lost my son. I lost my son to the war. A war that should never have happened; a war started by men who had a need for power where their hearts should have been; shame on them.

My son had been everything to me, everything. His father had died when he was just an infant, just a tiny child. He had no memories of his father, but I was able to supply him from the richness of mine. My son, my darling boy, joined the RAF. I was so proud, proud but fearful, dreadfully fearful that he might meet an untimely end. I would often ask him to remember his prayers. He would laugh and say, "Mother, don't worry so. I pray in my own way. I don't want to tempt fate."

When he was a small boy we would kneel by his bed together and he would ask God to keep his daddy safe in heaven, and to keep us safe here on Earth. I would always add a quiet word or two of my own asking an angel to watch over my lovely boy. I carried on doing that for years and years; in fact, when he joined up and went away to train and then to fight, I was doubling up on prayers several times a day.

I would hear from him now and then. He couldn't say what he was doing or even where he was sometimes, but I'd be content knowing he was safe for another few days. But then the news I had always been dreading. My boy—my precious, precious boy—had been shot down.

I was in terrible distress and shock for days. I didn't wash, didn't go out, I avoided callers. Such distress, such anger, such terrible, terrible agonising pain. I shut myself away from humanity. I didn't want to know life was continuing when my boy was dead. I didn't want to think, certainly didn't eat, and briefly sought solace in alcohol. I wanted to be free of this crucifying pain. I wanted it to be a lie, a dreadful unspeakable lie.

Surely, I thought, he must be coming home. He can't be dead, not my boy—not my boy, so vibrant, so youthful. His life couldn't be snuffed out so quickly, so harshly . . . and then I would look again at the telegram, and I would know it was true. I could not cope with the pain. It was too much for one body to bear. How, I wondered, was a person ever to stand upright again carrying such a weight of despair?

Gradually people began to filter back into the ruins of my life. Kindly people, but their company was no comfort to me. Their expressions of sorrow only heightened my own, and the crying would begin again. I told no-one of my plan to join my son and his father, whom I had loved very much. I had coped with his death because of my son; that reason wasn't there anymore, I didn't have to live. I had nothing left to live for.

He had no funeral, my son, a memorial service but no funeral. The sea had swallowed the remains of him and his plane, pulling them down to the ocean floor, resisting my need for a fitting resting place. I was angry about that—I had wanted him under the chestnut tree in the churchyard, beside his father, but that was denied us both.

I was filled with a consuming need to be with my husband and son. I willed myself to die. Every day I prayed to the Lord to take my soul, to take me out of that life; I willed it with every breath. I found I didn't have the courage to kill myself, I tried, I tried several times, but the fear of messing it up always stopped me at the brink.

Life eventually improved. After a long, long time I could mention my son without weeping. I could look at his photograph without sinking to my knees and howling at the sheer agony of loss. I emerged from two years of unremitting sadness and pain a different woman—I know I was— I felt different, inside and out. Grief changes you; real, raw grief leaves a scar on your soul. You live with it because, over time, it becomes a scar instead of the open wound it was, but you are forever changed.

My health began to fail, and in truth, I welcomed this. I still had days when I ached for the loss of my husband and son, days when I longed for their cheerful company.

I began to dream of my son. Sleep was my escape—in my dreams he would always be smiling and waving, always at a distance walking away from me, but turning and waving just before he vanished from view. Sometimes his father was with him, his arm around his shoulders, proud, laughing. I would wake, my face wet with tears, but, having seen them, I would gather the courage to begin another day. My faith, such as it was, sustained me. I would ask that the angels watch over my husband and son, and that when my time came I might join them.

I died in my bed. The house took a direct hit, blown to smithereens. All that was left was rubble and dust. I had gone to bed that night having said my usual prayers—I always talked to my boy and his father just before going to sleep. I would tell them about my day, tell them I loved them. This night was no different in that way, but I did feel a sense of expectancy. I put this down to the probability of another bombing raid and thought no more about it.

Death didn't frighten me: I welcomed it. I don't recall hearing the sirens, I don't recall anything at all from that night, except that when I opened my eyes I could scarcely believe what I was seeing.

"Hello Mother," he said, smiling that lovely golden smile he had. "Hello Mother, how are you feeling?"

I said, "I can see you!"

He laughed and said, "Of course."

"Oh, my boy," I cried, "I can see you. Am I dead? Am I really dead?" I couldn't believe it. I was dead! I was dead and I was with my boy. I cannot begin to describe the absolute joy in that moment, *the absolute joy!*

"There's someone else here," he said, "someone else to welcome you." He swept out his arm and there they were, side by side, the two men who had been the love of my life, for all of my life.

*Brenda's story is included because of the potency of her words,
and also in memory of my lovely friend
Rhona Alice Marsh
who on the stage, and in her own inimitable
style, brought Brenda's words to life,
and added hugely to my own life with her friendship,
fantastic humour, loyalty and love.*

*Everyone deserves a friend like Rhona.
If you have one . . . cherish them, because they are indeed a gift.*

Chapter 16

Jon

Jon came to me when I was driving home along a deserted country road late at night. In another life I may have driven off the road in fright. In this life, I am used to having company turn up in my car. I asked him to wait until I got home to tell me his story, because I don't carry a pen and paper in the car. He was happy to wait, and in fact at one point, told me to pull over tighter to the hedge because a blue car was coming around the corner in the middle of the road. I did so immediately, he was right.

I hit a bloody great tree and nearly turned the car over. I was a gonner in seconds. I didn't shout out, I wasn't lying there calling for me mum or nothing—she worried about that, I know she did. She used to torture herself thinking I was trapped there calling for her, but I never. I was right out of it. Last thing I remember is the tree coming towards me. I was going too fast and lost control on a wet bit of road, there was no other vehicle involved. At first they thought maybe I'd been racing someone and got pushed off the road or something, but no, it was my fault.

I was a speed freak. I used to like me lager, and I'd try a bit of dope now and again, but I liked speed best. It was the thrill of it, you know. I'd been speeding in cars since I was 14. Someone else driving then of course, but I'd egg them on to go faster and faster. There was endless complaints from folks on the estates. The police used to come out and give us a warning; soon as they'd gone we'd be at it again.

One night I decided I'd race a bit further out, try my skills in some country lanes, in the dark—how stupid is that? I don't know what I was thinking really, and looking back, I can see I was an idiot. Still, I died doing what I really loved. "Waste of a life." everyone said, but it was my life, and in the end I lived it the way I wanted.

I thought when you died that that was it, you know—when you're dead, you're dead—only it's not like that, see. Tell the truth, I never paid a lot of attention to what happens when you're dead; I mean I never paid no attention to religious stuff in school, religious education was dead boring. I got a hell of a surprise when I died, I can tell you. One minute I was in the car wrapping myself around a bloody great tree, then I was outside the car looking at it all.

I remember thinking, "What a bloody mess. They'll never get me out of that." Next second, and I mean really quickly, like I didn't have time to think it, I was heading off down this kind of tunnel. Well, it weren't a tunnel exactly—I mean I'd probably have been scared if I seen a tunnel when I knew I was on a road with loads of trees, don't make sense.

Anyway, I saw all these people in the distance, and I knew they were waiting for me. At first I thought it was me mates come looking for me, but as soon as I thought it I knew it weren't them.

Whoever it was, was on my side, I knew they were friendly. I was walking towards them and it was dead bright, you know, like daylight only brighter. And someone appears beside me, just like that, not creeping up on me or anything, they just appeared. I should have been scared, I mean there was no-one else about but me, it was the middle of the night.

This bloke appears and says, "Hello Jon," like he knows me.

I looks at him and says, "Who are you?" Only it didn't come out of my mouth, I heard myself say it, but it was like a thought. Weird.

Anyway, he says/thinks to me "I am your guardian angel."

Well, I laughed then, didn't I. I mean I knew I was dead, and here's my guardian angel. "Come on," I says, "you didn't do much of a job, did you? I mean, I'm flaming dead, ain't I?"

Give him his due, he didn't get mad or anything. He smiled at me and said it was my decision to drive like a maniac, he just had to make sure he was around to catch me when I did and ended up killing myself.

"Fair do's," I said, "so what now?"

"Now," he said, "we're heading in this direction" and pointed up ahead to all these folks.

"Who are they?" I said.

"Family," he said, "family and friends."

"But I don't know all my family whose dead," I said. "I only know a few."

"Don't worry about that Jon," he says, "they all know about you. They've been waiting. You nearly arrived early a couple of times." He was right too, I had a couple of near-misses before the biggie.

I met loads of people. Got to see how the family was affected by my death; that's how I knew about my mother torturing herself, and my grave with my picture on it, dead smart that is. Everyone goes and talks to the grave you know. I'm not in there—too depressing—looks good though. Mum put a little fence around it but the council told her to take it down . . . miserable bastards.

There was a lot of people at me funeral, never knew I was so popular. I 'spect a lot of 'em came to take a look. Lot of my mates there, which made my mum mad. She thought if it weren't for them leading me astray, I'd still be alive. But no-one led me astray, didn't need to; if anything, I did the leading. Dozy bugger I was at times, wouldn't listen to reason. But that's youth, in't it?

I'm all right now. I wasn't specially pleased to be dead, but it *was* my fault. I still get to ride in fast cars, I love it. The driver doesn't know I'm there though, which is just as well otherwise they'd be joining me quicker than they thought. I'm still a bit of a lad; even though I drove me mother mad she'd still like to hear that. I was a bit of a lad but I was *her* lad, I love her to bits. I never told her that 'cept when I was little. I used to tell 'er all the time then but when I got bigger I never said it as much. I used to give her a squeeze now and then but I wish I'd said it.

That's why I'm comin' now, to tell her, 'cause I know she'll read this one day, and she'll know it's me. I want her to know she's the best mum ever . . . ever, ever, ever. And I do hear her when she talks to me. It's important that, to get that across. Keep talking to us, everyone out there—we do hear you. We don't expect great long conversations, just, "Hello," or "I'm thinking of you," or "Goodnight," will do—means a lot.

CHAPTER 17

BRIDGET

Bridget's story touched me deeply. Her humour and her personality came shining through. This lovely young woman's story is truly a love story, in the fullest sense of the word.

I am Bridget, I was twenty-three when I died. Twenty bloody three, can you believe it? Cancer. A1 cancer of the blood. Leukaemia, I could never spell it—never wanted to get that close to it. I hated having it; it blighted my life—that's an understatement, isn't it? Bloody-well *ended* my life.

I'm okay about it now, not a lot of choice really, but I was angry at the time, bloody angry and all. I felt cheated, my family felt cheated. There was I at twenty-three, lots to live for, bright future and all that, then *bang*—cancer of the blood! Wasn't anything they could do, it'd gone too far by the time it was diagnosed.

I'd been ill for ages, on and off, gradually getting weaker and weaker until eventually some blood was taken—very poor quality I'd heard—and the bloody cancer was found. What a day that was.

We got a call to come into the surgery. I hardly knew my family doctor; I must have only seen him four times in ten years, so I could hardly relate to him. He was a nice enough chap but we didn't have a connection, you know. I think it's best to hear bad news from someone that knows you well, softens the blow a bit. Him telling me, well it was stark, you know, loud . . . final. Crystal clear—it was like he was talking to me from a tunnel, funny feeling, very weird. He was watching me intently when he gave me the news.

He was nervous, as though I might cause a scene or something and he wouldn't know how to deal with it. I was too shocked to cause anything like a scene; besides, I'm not the sort to go into hysterics, it's just not me. I retreat, go inside myself, try to digest what I've just experienced before I react to it. My mother, now *she* has scenes; she'd have had hysterics all over the place. That's probably why I'm like I am, and why I didn't take her to the surgery with me.

She was bad enough when I told her at home. We nearly had to have the paramedics out; she sort of yelped in shock then went into a dead faint. Dad looked at me, looked at her, burst into tears then didn't seem to know what to do. *I* had to sort Mother out. I put a cushion under her head then kept tapping her face and calling her until she came to, I was there for what felt like ages.

Dad kept saying, "Here, you sit down. I'll bring your mother round."

I said, "It's okay Dad, I can do it. You put the kettle on." He needed something to do.

I kept thinking if she doesn't come round in a minute I'll have to get an ambulance. After about ten minutes she stirred. Dad was there with a cup of tea, which didn't get drunk, and I just sat there waiting for her to be sensible enough to talk. She was quiet for ages, well it felt like ages, it was probably only a minute, if that.

She whispered, "What are we going to do?"

I said, "Why are you whispering?"

She replied, still whispering, "I don't know. Maybe because it's serious."

I laughed then. I mean, I know it wasn't funny, but whispering seemed right, as though we were in awe of this devastating news. If we whispered, it maybe lessened the devastation of it—daft what you do, isn't it?

I said I'd go for all the treatment I was offered, but even then, right at the beginning, I knew I wasn't going to make it. I don't know how I did, I just did. I didn't tell Mum and Dad that of course; I couldn't do that—they needed something to believe in. They came with me to see the consultant and were with me when I was given the news that it was terminal. Dad, bless him, took it well . . . well, as well as anyone could take the news that his only daughter was dying. Mother went into flat-out hysterics. She cried and carried on alarmingly; she had to be given a sedative she was in such a state. I felt embarrassed for the consultant. Dad just gave him a 'see what you've done' look. I couldn't get out of there fast enough.

I remember thinking, "Well, that's it for me then. Shan't worry about changing my job now." I'd been bored for ages. Let me tell you, there's limited scope for excitement in insurance. I'd been thinking of a change of career for ages but had never really looked into it seriously. Now I didn't have to—I was going to be an angel. I thought, "How's that for a career change? Can't get much higher up than that."

I told my friend Mary about that. She said maybe I was being over ambitious, that you probably had to have been dead a long time to be an angel. I said I'd go on the waiting list then. She said next time she was in church she'd put a word in for me, get me moved up the list a bit. She had connections, see—her mother's brother's godfather was a vicar, not that she knew him very well, in fact hardly at all, but because he was *nearly* a family member she was sure it would help. I knew I'd be waiting a while because Mary only went to church if someone was being matched or despatched.

I found out much later, after I'd died in fact, that once she'd had news about my health, Mary went into the church and said a prayer every time she went to town. I was stunned when I was shown all the prayers that had come in from Mary. We get to see, you know. After I arrived and had settled in, I got to see all the prayers that had been said for me—there were stacks and stacks. I was very touched, and somewhat peeved that they hadn't been answered, but it wasn't to be. It was my turn to come back and that was that.

I died pretty quickly after diagnosis; about nine months it was. Even that was longer than the doctors thought I would last. I died at home quietly with Mum and Dad and Mary. It was peaceful and very loving, just as I would have wanted it to be. I hated fuss. I wasn't quite ready to go, but my body left me no choice.

But I tell you what, I wasn't going to die a virgin—oh no, not if I could help it. I'd been saving myself, see, for marriage. It was how I was brought up and was right for me. But once I knew I was going to die I thought, "Right, I need to experience sex." Not just sex for the sake of it but lovingly, from someone who cared for me.

I remember sitting down with a notepad and pen and making a list of all the likely candidates—blokes I worked with, friends, even the chap in the paper shop who'd always winked at me when he gave me my change. I thought he had a twitch at first, then it dawned on me it didn't happen when he served Mary or my mother. Quite made my day after that. He was nice looking, nice teeth and all that, but I couldn't work out how I'd broach the subject. I mean, what would I say? "Can I have the paper, ten Silk Cut, and would you like my virginity?"

Mary howled with laughter when I told her. She said my first time ought to be with someone who really cared for me so we went back to the list. I crossed off all the men at work. Three were married, one was gay and the other two were far too young, so that left friends. I crossed off the ones with girlfriends—I didn't want to leave bad memories of me. That left two—Brian and Phil. I liked Brian a lot but we weren't close, not in the way that Phil and I were. Brian was a laugh a minute and a good friend but he wasn't strong in himself. I didn't think he'd cope well making love to a dying friend. It would've freaked him out. That left Phil.

To tell the truth, I'd never looked at Phil in a sexual way. He was just there . . . always, ever since second year in school. We used to lose touch here and there over the years but always caught up again. To be honest, I thought Mary liked him. She was always a bit flirty with him whenever he showed up, not that he seemed to notice mind you. I asked Mary what she thought about it being Phil, and God love her, she told me to go for it. She thought if anyone, it should be

Phil; she reckoned he had a soft spot for me anyway. I must say the idea grew on me very quickly; it had to, I didn't have that much time.

Once I'd decided on Phil I felt quite excited about the idea, but I didn't have the slightest idea how to ask him, or whether he'd be that excited about it himself. I didn't tell anyone else about my plan, only Mary. We planned endless scenarios: how to ask him, how to set the mood, but by the time I'd worked up the courage to ask him I was a complete wreck. I'd decided the best thing to do would be to have a meal, hopefully have enough to drink to be tiddly, explain what I wanted and hope he'd be so fired up by the compliment that he'd seduce me over the chocolate mousse . . . only it didn't happen like that.

We had the meal, that was fine. I told him about my diagnosis and somehow got round to my virginity—it took half a dozen red wines to do so. He took it very well, the news. He was shocked and upset of course, and hurriedly told me he was flattered I'd chosen him to take my virginity, but he'd have to decline the offer.

I was horrified, horrified and dreadfully embarrassed. Not, he said, because he wasn't attracted to me, far from it. He'd always been attracted to me, even when I had awful acne and an attitude to match—in my defence I was 14 and plastered in it. But, he said, he didn't want any relationship between us to be so organised—he would prefer things to be spontaneous.

I said, "Phil, I haven't got time to wait for you to be spontaneous. If you're not interested or it's too heavy for you to deal with, just tell me." I was getting angry by now, and I was as embarrassed as hell.

He was really good about it. He talked to me, told me I was special to him and maybe he hadn't explained himself very well because it was such a shock. He took me home, gave me a hug and I went to bed alone, feeling a complete fool and wondering if our friendship would ever survive it.

Mary called by the next morning hoping for the juicy details. You should have seen her face when I told her what had happened.

"What!!!" she yelled. I had to tell her to pipe down. I didn't want my mother hearing about my disastrous seduction routine.

I avoided any contact with Phil for about a week. I just couldn't have looked him in the eye without squirming. I thought he must have been avoiding me for the same reason. So when he turned up the next Saturday night I was really surprised. Even more so when he said to pack a few things because we were going away for a few days. I started to ask questions.

"No questions," he said, looking at his watch. "You have exactly half an hour to pack."

I was excited and very perplexed, but I was downstairs and ready to go in twenty minutes flat. I was so relieved that our friendship was intact that I would have done anything or gone anywhere. In that week when we'd not spoken I'd done a lot of thinking and had come to the conclusion that deep loving friendship was more important than sex, and that I'd just put thoughts of my virginity aside and not mention it again.

I said bye to Mum and Dad (who didn't look at all surprised by Phil's arrival, even though they tried to) and set off with him to I knew not where. We'd been going for a good five or ten minutes before I asked where we were going.

"Wait and see," he said, all mysterious.

My tummy was doing back flips and I had no idea why. Deciding it was a nice feeling of anticipation, I put on a favourite tape of ours and sat back to enjoy the ride. When I began to see signs for the airport I thought "Nah, can't be". When we turned into the airport car park, I said I hadn't packed my passport.

Phil said, "I know," and tapped his pocket, "your mum gave it to me a few days ago."

"You crafty bugger." I said.

Phil laughed and said, "Yeah, that's why you love me."

I didn't say anything, but I'll tell you what—it hit me like a bolt from the blue. He *was* right, I *did* love him. My tummy gave such a lurch I had to grab the door handle.

"You all right?" he asked, looking at me with concern in his eyes.

"Yeah," I said, "I'm fine. Where are we going again?"

He laughed and said, "You don't catch me out that easy. Wait and see, not long now."

We only ended up in New York. I can't begin to tell you what a wonderful time we had. We stayed in a dead posh hotel. I was struck dumb when I first walked in. It was *huge*; bigger and swankier than any building I'd been in before. The luxury—it was beautiful.

We had a fantastic meal, saw the sights, after I'd had one of my many naps that was. I could have slept during the flight as well, but we'd sat and chatted and covered a lot of ground—deep stuff. Phil told me he'd loved me for years and years, but had really realised it until the night I'd told him how ill I was. I couldn't tell him that I thought I loved him too; the words just wouldn't come. I wondered what was the matter with me. Struck dumb I was . . . not like me at all.

We had a wonderful, wonderful, time: four days of sightseeing and food. I was so tired at the end of each day that I slept like a log for hours and hours. We shared a bed but nothing happened. We kissed of course and held each other, but I'd always fall asleep. My body was just knackered, it was giving up on me. But the last night . . . wow!

The last night was magic, pure magic. We had a meal in the room, we sat on the balcony and looked for stars, we drank champagne, and we held each other and talked and talked . . . and then we loved. I will never ever forget that night. I won't go into details because it's private and was so special—I did tell Phil I loved him. It's important that people know that. I shall be forever grateful to him for loving me so beautifully.

Chapter 18

LISLE

This thoughtful child came in response to my asking, in the last days of putting this book together, if anyone else wished to be included. As usual the connection began with her telling me her name and me rushing to grab a pen and paper. All monologues are hand written first, that way I can keep up with the person talking and the images they show me before putting their story onto the computer. Half way through writing her story, the images I saw were haunting and graphic yet this little girl was concerned that I may be upset. "I just needed you to see" she said. "I'm sorry if I made you sad." Lisle was nine or ten years old, but the wisdom her spirit carries is ageless.

Hello, My name is Lisle. My papa was my hero you know; is my hero, he is with me now as I speak to you. He said it would be a nice thing to do to tell my story because it will help someone. He helped lots of people, but it got him into trouble. That is what I want to tell you about because Papa says even if it gets you into trouble, you should never regret helping people.

We got into lots of trouble, it was bad thing that happened to us. We are not sad anymore though, please do not think my story sad: although it is sad in one way, in another way we are all together and there is nothing sad about that.

We were all shot, one by one they shot us, the men. They shot my family and they made my papa watch. It was his punishment they said, his punishment was to watch, to watch his children and his wife, my mama, being shot, for helping other people. They held him back, those men, they held my papa and made him watch, until they had shot us all, then they shot him.

They shot my baby brother first, Mama was trying to shield him but they wrest him from her arms and put him on the floor. He tried to crawl back to Mama, they shot him in the back. What kind of a man shoots a baby in the back? Mama went out of her mind right there in the kitchen beside the stove, her mind just emptied, all that was left was a noise, just a wailing noise. The men, they wouldn't let her go to him, they held her arms behind her and made her watch, made us all watch as he twitched a little and died there in our kitchen in his own little pool of blood.

Three men aimed their guns at us, my sisters and I. I saw my sister spin and fall, my little sister so sweet and funny, she fell at my feet. I couldn't move. The shock was so terrible. I could hear my papa screaming our names. That was the last sound I heard as I left my body, my precious papa screaming our names and my mama, my dear mama losing her mind.

We were killed for helping our neighbours, how can anyone not help their neighbour? They were good people, farmers like us. Papa hid them in the barn, in the store under the barn, but they found them. They killed them by hanging them in the barn; after they did unspeakable things to Anna they hung them in our barn. Our barn that had only ever seen life, how could they do that? And then they came for us; there was no escape, we had no guns, we had nowhere to go. So many soldiers, so many soldiers for one small family. Not so brave, with their guns and their nasty ways, they were not so brave as my papa.

We are together now, we will always be together. But what of these men? How do they live peaceful lives knowing what they have done? I do not understand how ordinary men can be transported into different people, into evil people.

Papa told me that evil does not exist as an entity in itself; that is a myth. Evil is not separate from ourselves, we are not overtaken by it as some believe. He says evil is present in everyone. It is like a mad dog; if you provoke it, if you feed it more badness, it becomes more powerful—evil is madness dressed up as power. The madness has to be fed more and more until it feels mighty and untouchable, but when there is nothing left to feed on it will turn on itself and destroy the soul from the inside.

Papa says the souls who are eaten up with evil of their own doing, who have passed this way already, are in torment. They will not see us, they cannot reach us. We are safe now, we will always be safe from evil such as this. Papa says they have to face every evil act they had a part of, every evil act they sanctioned or did. They have to *feel* everything: he says this is a law and there is no escape.

I would not like to be these people; I feel sorry for them. Papa says this shows I am a good person, but they are lost to us; even if we wanted to help them we cannot, for they chose their path when they opened the door to evil.

That is my story, I hope it doesn't make you sad, I don't want people to feel sad hearing my story. Papa says it will help people and I believe him, because my papa never told a lie in his whole life. Thank you for listening to me, I have to go now. Papa says my work here is done and I will have helped a lot of people with my words, because it will bring them peace. I think it is important to be peaceful, don't you think? Everyone deserves a peaceful life.

CHAPTER 19

BETTY

This wonderful lady arrived in my kitchen as I prepared to wash the dishes after my children had left following a family get together. "Leave the dishes dear," she said, "I'd like to talk to you and I don't know how long I can hold this for." I got paper and pen, and there in my kitchen amid piles of unwashed dishes, Betty told me her story.

All I heard was a loud crack. I looked up to see this ruddy great tree falling, like it were in slow motion. It were falling on me! I didn't have time to move. I was stuck to the spot, then thunk! That were it—nothing but darkness. I don't remember feeling anything. I think I put me arms up to protect myself, but that was it. And how daft is that? As if putting me arms up would save me from a whackin' great tree, I ask you. Anyway, I died. That was it. And how undignified an' all, lying there under a ruddy great tree.

I tell you what, it's not the ending I would have chosen, far from it. I didn't mind it bein' quick and painless, but not in the open. I mean to say, I felt sorry for the poor folk who found me. You go for a walk after your Sunday lunch and you come across summat like that—I bet they never had tea that night.

The strange thing about this is that when it happened I didn't *feel* it. I don't know why, maybe because that's how it were planned. I have asked and were told that those who are going to die suddenly *don't* feel it. They are removed, their spirit is removed, seconds before impact so's they don't experience the trauma. I mean dying can be traumatic enough, and in some cases, it's certainly a surprise. It's like people falling from great heights—they're whisked out before they connect with the ground. Absolutely, and so it should be—they're going to die, so why put them through something that's of no benefit to experience. I can see the sense in that.

I was very lucky that I went suddenly, there's a lot to be said for it. Shocking for all the family to deal with though, all that sadness and things left undone. I had a casserole in the oven, it was fit for nothing by the time they found it. But overall, from *our* point of view, going sudden is a good death.

That's such a harsh and final word, death. It's not a death . . . it's a passing, a transition. And, if you did but know it, quite an adventure! I'm doing things now I never thought possible, I can go anywhere, see anyone I want to. We all can, it's very liberating. A great sense of freedom, no fear, absolutely no fear at all. It's an unknown word here, unless you've been a bad devil—then you've got some explaining to do. But that's in a whole different area, I don't go there. Apparently you can, if there's someone you know there, and you want to help them; I haven't been to look.

There's bound to be a certain person I know there, and in some ways, it's a relief he is, because I wouldn't want to meet him where I am. That would be too painful for me to deal with. Apparently he's got explaining to do, but first he would have to admit he was wrong, and if he's anything like he was when he was alive that will be a long time coming. I don't wish to see him suffer, I don't wish to see him at all. I was told that a man such as he will have to face what he did—no choice about that—and if he suffers through doing so that will not be my fault. He brought this on himself through the choices he made.

I'm just so glad I tried to do right by people. I didn't always get it right, and seeing your part can be a mite uncomfortable; but overall, I didn't do too bad. I saw the areas where I could have done better . . . choices made, lessons learnt and all that. Painful, funny, sad and happy all rolled into one—a very emotional but necessary experience. My greatest achievement was loving my family and being loved in return, and when you boil it all down there's nothing more important than that, nothing at all.

I miss them, I miss the physical closeness of them, but I visit. I hear them talk about me. I know they love me still—it reaches me, their love reaches me. It comes in waves and I stand there and soak up every last bit of it, and it makes me glad that I was a proper mum. I made all the sacrifices you do as a mother. That was my career, my choice, and I've never regretted a minute of it. I can see I sent them out into the world as good people, and I'll be here waiting for them when they come home; just like I always was.

Chapter 20

Jake

Jake was a loud, blunt, no nonsense character, who was intrigued at coming through to me, and was at pains to point out that an officer he served under was a 'fucking moron' who, he believed, had cost him and his friends their lives. Jake had lived and breathed army life and didn't see a reason why physical death should get in the way of continuing to do so.

We were ambushed. Had no chance—a hundred to one, might as well have been for all the chance we had. Bloody diabolical it was: insufficient ammo, insufficient arms, insufficient fucking brains. Not us, we were alright, it was the C.O—fuck all brains he had. God knows how he got to that rank—pillock. Took us right into a fucking ambush, gunfire like fuckin' rain—bastards.

I kept telling the others, "Let's get the fuck out of it!"

It didn't feel right to me see; where we were, it didn't *feel* right at all. Oh, I know it's drummed into us to obey orders, but this, his was an order to commit fucking suicide.

I was all for the off, but the others, they weren't going anywhere, proper army boys—trained them well. Me? I was always a fucking rebel. If there was a ruck you could bet your life I was in there somewhere, either sorting it or helping out. I was a right handy bugger, boxer see, loved me boxing—burned all the aggro off. Burned off all the frustrations of poxy orders that made fuck all sense.

We're taught not to question, to just obey—not possible for me, I question everything. Partly because some poxy officer has decided he wants to be a fucking hero. Trouble is, he would have laid down our lives like a fucking carpet on the way to get his medal. Some of them were decent officers, some of them made sense, some you'd willingly follow to the grave; but others, nah—I wouldn't follow them to the local shop.

I didn't get to see who shot us; none of us did, we were cut down in seconds, fucking seconds. I remember the feeling of falling, and thinking, "Fuck I'm falling," and that was it, like in slow motion. We all went down together—friends, even in death, eh? Funny thing was we were still there, saw Arabs swarming over us, but were strangely removed from it. Not distressed, surprised and confused, but not scared.

Just as the enemy began ransacking our bodies I noticed a light so intense, it commanded our full attention, and got it. We were sort of drawn into it, surrounded by it, held there, suspended.

I thought, "I don't know what the fucks happening here, but I might as well go with it," seemed like the thing to do. Then I see's someone coming towards us, I recognised him right off, it was our old sarge. He'd been killed months before, shot in the head by the bastards; morale hadn't been the same since, not really—he was a decent bloke. He snapped to attention in front of us, I couldn't fucking believe it.

I thought, "What the fuck?"

He laughed and said, "It's definitely me soldier, you can shut your mouth now."

I said, "What the fucks going on, Sarge?"

"You fucking died, Son" he says. "You all did, back there, ambush, nasty. Still, no good complaining about it, that's the risk you took when you joined up, better make the best of it, come along now. You're fucking heroes now you know—fuck all use to you here, of course, but it might help your families to cope a bit."

At the mention of our families, two younger ones panicked a bit and wanted to go back.

"Not possible," says the sarge, "This here's a permanent posting. Come on chin up, you signed on for a fucking adventure—that's what you were sold! Well, come on shape up—this is where the real adventure begins boys." He was fucking right too.

I never believed in life after death; well I never really thought about it. We didn't talk about dying, didn't want to encourage bad luck, but when your numbers up, it's up, there's no arguing with that.

But I wanted to let anyone who's lost someone in battle, I wanted to let them know that we always gather up our own. They always see someone they know, familiar faces and all that, makes a difference you know, seeing a familiar face or uniform, makes a big difference.

I like going back, I go back all the time. Army through and through I am, I like to help others still fighting out there. Give a nudge when they need it you know, help to keep them safe. Some of them are only kids, you know. I help them with their instinct, help them get the fuckers who got us.

Chapter 21

Liam

Liam was one of the first people ever to come through to me when I was taking dictation from spirit people for what would become this book, a little boy who in the midst of his life limiting illness thought only of his parents

When I died my Granfer came to get me—he came because he was the only person I knew who had already died. He was eighty-two when he died, his heart just packed up, he said. He sat on my bed for several days before he took me. My mum and dad couldn't see him, ever! I used to tell them all the time that he was there. Mum used to get all teary, and Dad would just start talking about something else, like football or something. Granfer said it was okay, not everyone could see him, only special people. He only appeared to special people.

I said, "What about Mum, isn't she special?" She was his daughter.

He said, "Yes, well, your Mum *is* special," but, he explained, it wasn't her time to go on a trip with him, it was mine—*that's* why I could see him, *that's* what made me extra special he said. When it was Mum's turn he'd make sure she felt special too.

I thought, "Oh, that's all right then."

Granfer smiled a lot. Sometimes he held my hand in the night when I was a bit scared. He would just know and there he would be on my bed. Sometimes he brought Percy; Percy was his cat, a ginger cat. He got run over by a milk lorry right outside Granfer's gate, it was a tragedy. Granfer said Percy was a pain in the neck sometimes, because he never stayed still long enough to come with Granfer on every visit. That's why I only saw him and felt him snuggle down on my bed about two times.

I was never scared when Granfer was there. I was more scared about my mum and dad. They weren't talking very much, and Dad was living at Nan's. They tried to be all happy when they visited me but I knew they were only pretending. I asked Granfer about it one time; he said they loved each other really, but they had some things to sort out.

"It's like when you have a disagreement with your friends in the playground. You call each other names, then sulk for a bit, then you're friends again . . . all your disagreements forgotten," he said. "Well, your mum and dad are at the sulking stage. They'll be all right in a little while."

I asked him if they'd be all right by the time I went with him to Heaven.

"No," he said, "but it would be very shortly after." I felt happier then; I wanted Mum and Dad to be happy again.

"They'll miss me though, won't they Granfer?" I asked him.

"Oh yes," he said, "they'll miss you for a long, long time; but they'll miss you together."

I was a bit teary then. I said "But Granfer, I'll miss them. I'm not sure if I want to go to Heaven."

He put his big old hand on my shoulder and looked right in my teary eyes and said "Ah, but that's what makes you extra special my boy. You can come back and visit any time you like. I will even bring you myself."

I felt much better about it all then, and asked Granfer if we'd have some adventures in heaven. I missed having adventures because of my sick heart. I used to love to go to the woods with Dad and my friends. We built a super fantastic den once, but some big boys smashed it down. Granfer said we would have lots of adventures—he would guarantee it.

I told Mum about my talks with Granfer—she said it sounded just like him. She said how did I know about Percy? Percy had died before I was born.

"I know," I said, "Granfer told me." She smiled at me a bit funny and then took my temperature.

I told her one day that Granfer was coming to take me to Heaven. She wasn't very pleased at the news.

"It's all right," I said, "Granfer said I can visit you anytime, but my heart is very sick. It can't be made better—it's just one of those things." Mum asked me when Granfer was coming again. I told her he'd be there the next night so she said she'd stay all night, because she'd like to have a word with Granfer, she wanted to see him for herself. I was just glad she believed me after all.

It was very dark when Granfer arrived; Mum was sleeping in the chair holding one of my hands. I felt him arrive and blow on my face to wake me up.

"Ssshhhh," he said, "don't wake your Mum." Well, I accidentally did. She shot up in the chair and grabbed my hand tight. Granfer was stood in the corner watching us.

"He's there," I said, pointing to him. Mum looked but she couldn't see, even with the light on she couldn't see him. I could, plain as day. He smiled and waved at me before disappearing.

"Oh," I said, "he's gone and I don't know what he was going to say to me." Mum said she'd had a dream that Granfer had come into the room. I said it wasn't a dream, he was really there. I got all teary and annoyed because he'd gone.

Mum said, "If it was important he'll come again."

Two days later I was really, really sick, I mean really *really* sick. I just lay there like a cabbage. I said it to Mum, and she went all funny.

"What did you say?" she said.

I said, "I'll just lay here and spread out like a cabbage." I don't know why I said it.

Mum said Granfer used to say that all the time. When he was tired he'd say "I think I'll just lie down and spread out like a cabbage."

Mum and Dad stayed with me. I got so sick I just slept all the time. I know it was 3 o'clock because my clock said so—I had a clock with hands that glowed in the dark. Mum and dad were asleep, Mum in the chair and Dad on the floor. I was very groggy but I could see Granfer peer at Dad then sort of step over him to come to my bed.

"Well well sonny boy, are you ready for an adventure?"

I said, "Yes please Granfer, I'm fed up being in this bed. Will we go far?"

"Oh, not very far," he said, "but far enough to have a very good time." He said all I had to do was take hold of his hand and hold on tight.

That's what I did. I felt a funny pulling feeling in my chest, like someone was sucking me out with a vacuum-cleaner, then *pop* . . . I was with Granfer. I looked back and saw me on the bed as well. I did look really sick but I was so thrilled to be with Granfer that I didn't think of anything else. We seemed to be flying very fast. I could see stars and lights and everything. Other people were with us, some going faster than us.

"Are they on an adventure too Granfer?" I said.

"Yes my boy," he said, "they most certainly are!"

Chapter 22

Valerie

Valerie was a worldly wise young woman, who through choice or circumstance, gained a living through the sale of her 'services'. She was as voluble in her speech after death as she was, no doubt, in life; managing to be both funny and incredibly poignant.

I turned tricks for a living, if you can call it that—most of the time it was a flamin' miserable existence.

I didn't have the intelligence or looks to go big-time: I had to make do with whatever flotsam came my way. Most of the time it was in the shape of pot-bellied old blokes. Some of 'em used to have a moan that they didn't get it from their wives anymore. I used to look at 'em and think, "Well, I'm only 'aving yer cos yer payin' me." What is it with men? Think they can let themselves go to pot and women will still fancy 'em—dozy buggers.

Occasionally I'd get a nasty one. One of 'em 'ad me with a knife once, long time ago. I wised up quick after that. Gave me a bloody fright, but not enough to put me off the game. Couldn't . . . I had a habit to support.

I was always afraid of death. I knew it would come for me early—didn't know how, just thought it would happen in an alley somewhere. I couldn't imagine me as an old lady, the lifestyle I had didn't allow for old age. I thought death would come quietly, slidin' in alongside a knife in the back or ridin' on the coat-tails of bad coke; but no, when death came for me it was roarin' like a bloody lion.

I was caught up in a three-car pile-up. The bloke I was with, a punter, was lookin' for somewhere secluded. The punters I usually had already had a place sussed, but not this one. He was really nervous, a first-timer, so we're drivin' round and around lookin' for a place. I gave him a few helpful suggestions, I mean arse-end-up against a farm gate was about the best of it, but he was so nervous he could barely think straight. I thought I'd just shut up and enjoy bein' in the warm and dry for a bit when he starts speedin' up, sayin' something about he's thought of a good place.

'Course, he wasn't concentrating like he should've been, anticipation and all that. This poxy car comes from outta nowhere, cuts us up. We hit the car in front, they swerve across us and another goes up our backside. It was a bloody mess, a bloody mess. I remember the grinding noise of metal on metal and the screamin' of tyres tryin' to grip the flamin' road—all noise and colour, colour and noise, so fast, no time to be scared.

I came around in the ambulance and wanted to know where me bag was. Not whether I 'ad all me arms and legs, just worried about me bag. Funny what's important, in't it?

I copped it right there in the ambulance; heart packed up right there and then. All I knew was that someone put the lights out, no pain, no nothing. Least I was in the right place, but they couldn't do nothing for me, I was past savin'. I heard them say something about haemorrhage. I saw me lyin' on the bed thingy. I was standing beside it while the ambulance men did all kinds of stuff to me.

I heard one say, "She's gone".

I thought, "No I 'aven't—I'm here, I'm all right."

Next thing I know I'm movin' really fast and I can hear me dad's voice; he died when I was a nipper.

He's calling my name, saying "Come on Valerie, we're waiting. Stop hangin' about."

I looked around me but couldn't see him, couldn't see nothin', then all of a sudden there he was. There was my dad, just like I remembered him, just as he looked when I was a kid. I tell you, it was like flamin' Christmas all over. The love I felt was so thick, I was kinda surrounded by it you know, lovely.

Soon as I saw him, my dad, soon as I saw him I was worried he'd be ashamed of me 'cause of the life I had. He looks at me all loving, holds out his arms and says, "Come here Val, come here to your old dad. It was your life." He said as he wrapped his arms around me, "The choices you made were your own. No-one sits in judgement of you here. Welcome home kid."

CHAPTER 23

IAIN

Iain had been afraid to die, afraid that what he had been told by religious people would be true, that he wouldn't be acceptable to God because he was gay. Happily this was not so, and he wanted to allay the fears of others who may, deep down inside, have this fear.

I died of AIDS—a long, slow, lingering death. It was harder for those who loved me than for me. I lay beside the big picture window looking out over San Francisco Bay. Some days the light was too bright and I'd have the blinds down, but most of the time I could just lay there and watch the boats and the people going about their daily lives, wishing I was one of them.

The drugs made me feel like a zombie. I tried not to take them all but I needed them, my body needed them—it was dying on me. Oh the frustration, my mind usually so pin sharp but my body was a wreck. My body was ugly and thin, so thin, and weak. I couldn't move for myself. Daniel fed me, helped me drink, helped me to urinate. Eventually, he didn't have to do that. He felt redundant; I felt redundant. Now and then I mused as to whether this disease was God's punishment for not living a (so-called) normal life. I had a letter in the early days, from some anonymous moron, telling me it was punishment—can you believe that? I dismissed it at the time as a fucked-up crank, but those words echoed round my brain now and then, so I guess their intentions had the desired effect.

I was never a bad person. I just loved a man, that's all. Love your fellow man, Jesus said, right? I said this to Daniel once and he said, "Yeah but I don't think he meant literally. Love them, he said, not *make love* to them." Daniel always had a problem with my promiscuity; he was a one-man guy. Me, I always went at life as though there wasn't enough time or enough men; I guess I paid the ultimate price for that.

I died on a Tuesday. Daniel had just washed me, as gently as he could. I had no part in the process but it exhausted me anyway. He said he had to go to the drugstore and would I be okay? I waved a feeble wave, he kissed me and was gone. I felt so, so tired—too tired, too ill to even glance out of the window. The blinds were half drawn against the bright sunlight that by now hurt my eyes.

I don't know what made me look toward the door. I wasn't even aware I could still move my head; it felt like a ton weight, so I'm not sure I moved it at all. I just remember looking at the door, watching it open. At first I thought Daniel had come back for something, but the person who came in wasn't Daniel. I don't know why, but I wasn't afraid. You think you would be if a stranger entered your room. I wasn't in the least afraid; it was as though a spell had been cast. The very air in the room felt different, weighted, expectant.

This person—I don't know to this day if they were male or female—was surrounded by light, intense but very serene light. I remember thinking this is it, I'm going to die. What's more, I wasn't in the slightest bit afraid of the notion either, very strange. The figure came to my bed and put their hand on my heart. I was filled with a warmth and love; *Jesus*, I'd never felt love like it. Every miserable little cell in my body was vibrating with it. I knew then that I was in the presence of an angel. Strange or funny as it might sound to some—and I would have been the first to laugh it off if someone told me they'd seen one—here was a real live angel. I knew it in my soul, and was filled with wonder. I don't recall seeing wings at all, and he/she didn't look anything like they do in the movies, but I was in the presence of an Angelic Being.

The Angel spoke to me inside my head, like hearing a thought—telepathic. I was told it was my time to enter the spiritual worlds.

I thought, "Wow, it's not true then. I *am* going to heaven after all." The relief was absolute, because I'd worried more than I'd admit that maybe, just maybe, I was headed to hell for being gay.

This feeling of love increased until I felt I wouldn't be able to stand it and that it would kill me. I heard the Angel tell me to sleep.

"Sleep?" I thought. "There's an Angel in my room doing God knows what to my heart and he tells me to sleep. Not a chance." I didn't want to miss any of this.

I fell asleep anyway, or was put to sleep somehow, because the next conscious thought took place in heaven—in the spiritual world, whatever you want to call it. I woke up in hospital. It was explained to me that I was now in what I called Heaven. The relief was so great that I cried like a baby. I was accepted and loved for being me, not judged by my sexual preferences.

So you tell them out there God doesn't hate you if you're gay. That's it really, that's what I wanted to say, because there are people still in fear. People shouldn't live in fear of death, so I wanted to come through to say that. Don't believe anyone who tells you that you're going to hell. Hell doesn't exist . . . it's a club people use to beat you with, to scare you into submission, into their way of thinking. It's a crock of shit, an unbelievable crock of shit. I don't get that—why would anyone want to scare people unless they got some power kick out of it. Warped, that's what a lot of people are, warped. Sad really, sad because they're missing out.

My life was my life—wonderful, fun, loving, partying, living. I wish I'd been more careful but it's easy to think that now. I accept my choices caused me to die but I'm cool with it. I just wanted to say that . . . to tell you, to tell others that being gay is ok. Don't fight yourself, and don't listen to nuts telling you you're going to hell. It doesn't exist. Remember I told you that—hell doesn't exist, ok?

That is all I wanted to say really—I just don't think people should be afraid. Too many people listening to fuck-ups, excuse my language, but that's what they are you know, someone fucked them up somewhere along the line, so they keep passing it on, idiots.

I don't want people like me, gay people, to have any fear. Dying when your imagination is running riot can be scary enough, without having some nutball in your head as well. I just want people to know that—I feel so strongly about it that I wanted to do this, too many scared people and not enough time eh? Thanks, thanks for giving me the time to do this. I hope it helps.

CHAPTER 24

KARIS

Karis was a darling girl who appeared to be around nine years old when she passed from this life. She gave her story in the hope that it will help those who have had people taken from their lives at the hands of another.

I am Karis. My daddy shot me. He shot my mom and my sisters too. I don't know why he did that. My mom always said Daddy was real sick, sick in his head. She said he'd been that way since he was a boy. His folks lived way back in the country, swamp-lands, Mom said. She said they wasn't right in the head either but she thought the madness had gone past Daddy. She said she sure was wrong about that.

Daddy turned real sick when he hit thirty-five; something just kinda snapped in his head. He thought we all was leaving him. We was only goin' to Grandma's, "for a little holiday" Mom said. But Daddy turned up real mad just as we was loading the truck, he was yellin' at Mom. She told us to get in the truck. I had to help my sisters in 'cause their legs wouldn't reach. It was a big ole truck, and they only had stumpy little legs.

I saw Daddy hit Mom, she went down on the ground, but got up again real quick. She waved at me tryin' to let me know everything was fine, like she just tripped or somethin'; but I knew it wasn't fine. Nothin' was ever fine again. I saw Daddy hit Mom again, least I think he did. I saw his hand raised then they went behind the house, like Mom was leading him away so we didn't see. But we'd seen him hit her before, usually right after he hit the bottle too. He was a changed man when he'd been at the spirits.

I heard the shot. My sisters heard the shot and began bawling their heads off. It was like we kinda knew what he had done. Afore long he returned to the truck where we was all of a heap. I tried to shush the girls. Daddy gets in the truck and begins to drive us away. I saw all the front of his shirt was ripped and there was what looked like blood there but I couldn't be sure. Coulda been sweat, he sure smelt like it.

I asked him in a trembling voice, "Was we going to Grandma's?"

"Nope," he says, spitting at the window, "we ain't going to Grandma's ever again."

Well I tried not to cry then but big hot tears came anyway. I loved my grandma a lot. I asked where Mom was, why'd we leave her behind. He said she had chores to do and we would meet up with her later. I asked where we was going, and Daddy backhanded me for askin' too many dumb-fool questions—that set the girls going again.

He pulls over real sharp—the tyres was screaming when we hit the dirt. He gets out of his side, opens our door and begins slapping us all, and yellin' fit to bust about how we's so ungrateful, trying to leave him, and other stuff I can't repeat 'cause most of it was cuss words. I knew I had to calm him down like I'd seen Mom do a hundred times.

"Daddy," I yells, "Daddy we love you. You're a good man Daddy, a good man."

You know what? He began to listen. First he began to cry then he began to listen. I told him we wanted to be with him, how he was the best Daddy in the whole wide world. My voice was shakin' as much as my knees but I seemed to be getting through. He quit hittin' us and sat down in the dirt with his back to our side of the truck. He was cryin' and sniffin', saying all kinds of crazy stuff. I could smell the drink, he was stinking of it.

The girls was quiet by now, just sniffin' and askin' for Mom in real quiet voices. I was watchin' Daddy. I had a feeling he'd done something bad. It was just a feeling, a 'watch out' kinda feeling. I felt a bit crazy in my head; I didn't know what to do. I figured maybe we should go back to the house and I offered to drive us back if Daddy was tired.

"What?" he yells, "I ain't tired. Besides we can't go home."

I didn't understand, but I just knew not to ask. Daddy was strugglin' with something and it had hold of him real tight. He gets up, brushes off the seat of his pants, and gets back in the truck. The girls asked where we're going.

"Are we goin' home? We want Mom." I shook my head at them to quit it which they did. That surprised me because usually they just go on and on but there was a strange feelin' in the truck, it made us all quiet.

I realised we was on the road to Grandma's and wondered if Daddy was taking us there after all. We never said nothin'. We pulled up in front of Grandma's house and Daddy told us all to get inside and see your precious Grandma. We didn't need no second telling, we was out of the truck and in that house faster than a jackrabbit.

Grandma was out the back planting peas and looked real surprised to see Daddy. We was sent back in the house to get milk and sultana cake while they talked; only I don't recall any talkin'. I heard yelling then another shot, I nearly jumped out of my skin. I told the girls it was someone shooting crows, but I knew it weren't.

Daddy came into the house and said we was better off with Mom and Grandma, 'cause where he was goin there wasn't room for us, we was too damn good. Then he shot us, all of us. Just the one time each, that's all it took. I remember lookin' down at this little hole in my chest, that's all I recall.

Next second I was standing there in Grandma's kitchen-diner, and a lady appeared. She was all in white and had a light all around her. She held her hand out to me and I took it. My sisters were there she said, they were just a little way ahead of us with Mom and Grandma. If we hurried we could catch them up. We seemed to pass through the house without moving. I know I didn't walk out, just kinda floated, I guess you'd say.

I met with Mom and Grandma. I met with a whole bunch of people what was my relations and such. I asked about Daddy, that's when Mom told me he was sick in the head. She said he'd be joining us later but he had some explaining to do to God first. Everyone had to explain why they'd done bad things, and not everyone is ready to see they were wrong, so it could be some time before we see him again.

We're still waiting.

Chapter 25

Chris

Chris gave me a funny, insightful and incredible account of what it was like to be in a coma, half way between this world and the next. His insightful, humorous and moving account will be of enormous help to others when faced with this heartbreaking scenario.

I was dying for a long time, a long slow process that was quite boring most of the time. I was in a coma, a 'persistent vegetative state' they called it.

No-one knew what to do for the best. I was breathing unaided at first, so it was thought that I was still in there somewhere. And sometimes I was, but as I've said, it was very boring.

On occasions I was aware of family visiting, talking to me, playing music, and even pinching me to see if there was a response. My sister was the one pinching me, not nastily, just the back of my hand, hoping I'd respond in some way. She caused uproar once, because my eyelid flickered. She thought I was showing signs of life, but it was just a muscle twitch. She used to sit and talk to me: tell me about the family, what everyone was doing. I remember she had a red raincoat; I know this because when she was talking to me I was very often behind her.

I could leave my body at will—a fantastic feeling. My parents would visit and my father would look at me and say, "He's not in today." He was always right. I felt frustrated in not being able to communicate with the family. I could see them but they couldn't see me—all they saw was this lump in the bed wired up to god-knows-what.

There was a lot of argy-bargy between the medical staff and my family. Some thought the machines should be switched off, and I'd be behind them saying, "Yes please". Then my family—my mother actually, bless her heart—wanted them to give me a bit longer, hoping against hope I'd come around. My body was too gone for that; she knew it really but wasn't ready to come to terms with it. I understood completely, and to be honest, it was a bit of a novelty being able to come and go as I did.

My dad used to bring a bar of Fruit-and-Nut and the crossword when he visited. He'd ask me for clues and I'd try to think the answer into his head. Sometimes he'd get it and would look surprised.

He'd say things like, "I swear I can hear you Son, now how about five across?"

Dad used to come on his own a lot. He'd chat away, believing that I could hear him, and I could. He even brought in a Millwall shirt once to see if it would provoke a reaction. If I could have, I'd have chucked it out the window—that would have made them jump.

Eventually I had trouble breathing; well, I didn't but my body did. A decision had to be made about keeping my body alive. They did all kinds of tests and I didn't react. I couldn't because I wasn't in there, I was watching from three feet away. It was quite interesting, in a detached kind of way.

I forgot to tell you—all the time part of me was in that coma, I kept being visited by my Nan and Gramps, and my mate Rob who'd been killed on his bike, motorbike that is—head injuries, nasty.

Anyway, he turned up one day by my bed and says, "You coming out for a look around then?"

Next thing I know I was wandering about the room as easy as you like.

"Brilliant," I thought, "I'll have some of this!" Then I sees Nan and Gramps, real as anything. Nan told me I'd have to wait a bit to be with them properly, on a permanent basis, but they'd be coming to get me regularly. Breaking me in I suppose.

I used to go off round the hospital with Rob, having a look at folks. There was all kinds of coming and going—babies, old folk—all kinds. I used to wonder if anyone could see us; Rob said only the ones that had died—we'd wave to each other as we passed, just like regular folks. Funny to think of it now, I wasn't in the least scared, not one bit, fascinated but not scared.

I always knew, always *felt*, when someone was coming to see me, so I'd nip back to my room to have a listen—to feel their love for me. I didn't like it in the early days when they were always crying. I wanted to let them know I was fine—not to cry, what's done was done—but it's hard.

I was really pleased when the machine was switched off. My parents did it together—Mum said they brought me into the world, they should see me off, quite right too. It was brave of them: took great strength on their part. That's how much they loved me . . . they set me free.

Nan and Gramps and Rob were in the room, just waiting. I was so pleased to be with them, so pleased to be free. You tell them, for anyone else in my position, there's nothing to be afraid of. Leaving your body is easy—that's all you do, leave your body. The love is still there, forever. It's the love they have for you that sets you free. You make sure they know that . . . please, make sure everyone knows that.

Chapter 26

Gavin

Gavin could never be described as a wallflower, His use of profane language extended his story considerably, but without it this just wouldn't be a true representation of Gavin, and every story and every person deserves to be heard. Gavin, very funny in the recounting of his exploits, has an extremely powerful message.

Hi, I'm Gav, or Gavin as me muvver said. She 'ated anyone callin' me Gav—said it was common. According to her, only common people did drugs; so I was as common as you could get, 'cause I took anything I could get my hands on.

Fuckin' heroin got me in the end, kept me goin' for years that stuff did. Course, I 'ad to nick anything I could lay me hands on to pay for it. I nicked me muvver's stereo, telly and video three times. She couldn't get insurance in the end; I feel bad about that now. I did loads of thievin'—I'd nick anything, and I mean anything, just for a measly few fuckin' quid. Pathetic it was, fuckin' pathetic; when I look back now and see how I was, it makes me fuckin' cringe.

'Course, I got to see it all after I copped it like. Fuckin' scary I can tell you! I didn't want to look, but you 'ave to, got no choice. Got to look back before you can look forward. I used to rob old ladies, anyone that looked as though they couldn't run after me. I was never violent like, not to people or dogs, only to property.

I did burglaries all over the place. I robbed me sister's once, but her old man caught me in the kitchen. He cracked the back of my head open with a bit of four-by-two, he was doing DIY at the time. I was on my knees when he hit me.

"Take that you little bastard," he shouts, then whack! I thought me brains was comin' out me fuckin' eyes. He yanks me up by me hood and yells, "Let's take a look at you, you little shit." Then he sees it's me and says, "Fuckin' 'ell Gav, you little bastard. If I'd known it was you I'd 'ave whacked you harder. Someone ought to put this family out of its fuckin' misery by finishing you off." He emptied me pockets of their money and his phone, then he clomps me round the ear for good measure.

Me 'ead was bleedin' all down me neck. I felt it and says, "I'm bleedin' Sid, I'm fuckin' bleedin'." He weren't fussed at all.

"So?" he says. "Then fuckin' bleed outside and not on my floor." He opens the front door and throws me out. I lands on my arse and he stands over me hissing. "You show your face round 'ere again, you little shit, and you'll be a fuckin' dead man. That clear? Next time it won't be a bit of wood, it'll be the carving knife." He stepped back and said, "I'm only letting you go now out of respect for your sister, not that you have any, you bag of shite. Now piss off."

I was only too glad to go, he frightened the hell out of me most of the time. I only went to rob their place because I'd heard me sister say they'd be away for a few days. I must've got the days wrong. My head was fuckin' hurting, but I daren't go to Casualty. What would I say? So I went home and stuck a towel round it 'til it stopped bleeding. 'Course, in the morning I 'ad to take the towel off, and it was all stuck to me 'ead—takin' it off made it bleed again, and I 'ad a lump the size of an egg for days.

Taught me though, I never went there again and he never mentioned my little nocturnal visit. He used to give me the look though, it was a "one foot wrong and I'll fuckin' 'ave you" look. I stopped robbing me muvver's around the same time. Being nice to people like me was the wrong thing to do. People like me—addicts— they just take advantage of that. I can see that being clumped by a big bastard like 'im was the only thing that did work. A good dose of fear—works every time. Least, it stopped me robbin' family; I just robbed other people instead!

Later on I got into dealing. That way I got my own stuff for free. Trouble is, I couldn't stay at the simple stuff, I 'ad to 'ave heroin. I'll call it heroin for you 'cause you won't be familiar with all the other names it's got, there's a list as long as your fuckin' arm. Anyway, I'd been dealing in this for months; I knew the coppers had an idea. They cruised past my place often enough, and I knew it weren't for the view, I knew I was pushin' me luck.

I was doin' too well at it when I got raided. Fuckin' hell, I thought the world was caving in, next thing I knew there's cops everywhere—couldn't fuckin' move for 'em. I was allowed to get dressed, and then I 'ad to stand in a corner while they turned the place over. I realised they'd find my heroin in no time; I'd hid it in the bog. I only had an ounce left 'cause I was expecting a delivery, but that ounce could've got me hung.

I said I needed to shit. They tells me to shut the fuck up, so I says, "If you don't let me go to the bog I'm going to do it right here and you can fuckin' watch." I'll tell you what, it was easy to shit myself—I was fucking scared enough. They ignores me so I pulls my trousers down and starts to squat. Still they ignores me, so I start to squeeze a bit out. All of a sudden one of them yanks me up by the hair and pushes me into the toilet door.

"Get in there you filthy little bastard. I don't want to see you fucking shit. You got two minutes."

I've never moved so fuckin' fast. I dumped my load—fastest shit I ever had—and got me heroin from its hiding place. Wrapped in clingfilm it was. I had to flush some away 'cause there was too much but the best of it I shoved up me arse. I know, what a fuckin' picture that conjures up—told you I was pathetic. S'prising what you can shove up your own arse when there's twenty coppers baying for your blood.

They found a load of E's, so I was taken into custody. You try walking with your cheeks together, it ain't easy. I kept thinking if I cough or sneeze, I'll lose the lot. Then I thought, I'll be okay 'cause I've got tracksuit trousers on, what a thing to think about. But it was fuckin' uncomfortable, I can tell you that for nothin'? I'd greased the package with a bit of soap, you know, that runny stuff—a girlfriend left it once, don't think I'd ever used it before, I don't know what they put in that soap, but it was bloody stinging.

Anyway, I'm in this cell for fuckin' hours.

"We'll get you a brief," they says . . . like hell! I was waitin' for fuckin' ever.

I don't know how long it was before I started to feel funny—very sick, very, very strange. I lay there on the bed, if you can call it that, fuckin' hard it was. I must have slept or something, because I opened one eye to see a funny little thing, sat in the corner of my cell looking at me.

Fuckin' ugly it was, like a little gremlin, sort of dark greeny grey, almost black. It blinked at me with its fuckin' buggy eyes; I shut me eyes and looked again. It was still there. I thought, "I'm fuckin' hallucinating, gotta be." I looked again, still there. Then it suddenly moved a bit which made me fuckin' jump, I can tell you.

I thought, "I'll wave to it, and if it waves back I'll know it's really there." So I waves, and it fuckin' waves back! I thought, "Fuckin' hell, it's a fuckin' demon come to get me." I very nearly shat meself there and then. It edged a bit closer, like it sensed my fear, I shouted to it to fuck off out of it. "You're only in me fuckin' head," I shouted, "You're not fuckin' real. Now piss off!" It fuckin' smiled. It fuckin' smiled, I tell you. "You understood what I just said, didn't you?" I says to it. It only fuckin' blinked at me with its fuckin' buggy eyes. "Are you from the devil?" I said to it. Blink fuckin' blink. Well, I got the shits then all right, big time.

It was about then that I realised the fuckin' heroin up me arse was in my system; I was ODing. Fuckin' weirdest feeling, brilliant and fuckin' scary; and all the time this fuckin' ugly bastard is staring at me. To tell the truth, I wasn't sure if I was fuckin' dead already. It was a weird feeling, like I was half there and half wasn't, you know, weird.

I can remember hearin' myself praying. Now, I've never fuckin prayed in my life, not real, honest-to-God praying. I've said, "Please God, don't let me get caught," if I'm robbing some poor bastard, but I don't think that counts. I was scared, *fuckin' scared!* I just knew the little bastard was coming for my soul. Suddenly all the things I'd done to people over the years came into my head. I thought, "What the fuck's goin' on 'ere?" and then I saw he'd edged closer.

"Fuck off," I heard myself shouting. "I'm not coming with you so you can fuck off out of it!"

It wasn't long before I felt someone else come into my cell; not so much come in, as arrive. A different feeling altogether—calmer, warmer. I felt as if I was torn between these two people, if you can call them people. I only heard a voice with the good feeling; it wasn't a man's or a woman's voice, just a voice. Whatever it was, the ugly bastard didn't like it—he went back to his corner making a funny hissing sound. The lovely feeling filled the whole cell; it was like brilliant light but it wasn't, weird.

I just knew I had a choice. No one told me, it just fell into my brain. "Make your choice."

I thought, "Fuck that, if I'm dying, which I surely was, then I'm not going to the fuckin' devil, not if I can help it."

I thought again of all the people I'd wronged: my family, everyone I'd shat on time and time again—I felt very sad about it. I asked this voice to help me, help me put things right if I could, I was dead sorry. I noticed that every time I said how sorry I was—and I really meant it with all my heart, 'cause I did have a good one in there somewhere, it was just silted over with all the drug use—every time I said sorry, the ugly bastard seemed to fade a bit.

"Fuckin' right on," I thought, "I can fuckin' do for you." Soon as I went back to even a little bit aggressive, he got stronger. It was like I was fighting myself—fuckin' Class A weird!

I fell on my fuckin' knees. I prayed to God (go to the top, I say!) I just hoped he was listening, because I needed him bad: I needed help from anyone who could be bothered. I never believed in God, not really. I mean, he was easy to blame for things, but I never thought he existed. But if he did, I needed him now. I said all this to him, I thought I might as well be upfront about it. I had nothing to lose except my soul, to the ugly little bastard, and I was goin to do everything I could to stop that happening. I told God what an evil bastard I'd been over the years. Looking back now, I know he already knew that; he had a list of my crimes as long as your fuckin' arm, and then some.

I died that night. The cling film up my arse ruptured, and the heroin went right into my system and killed me—fitting end really. I knew it would kill me in the end, I just didn't know I'd 'ave a battle for my soul to deal with. There's many a demon living with a druggie, just waiting, goadin' them on. If they knew, if only they knew the fight that was waiting for them, they might think twice about getting involved with the filthy stuff. But I doubt it: I wouldn't 'ave listened—I'd ave thought they was talking out their arse, but now I know different.

The good guys got me in the end, thank Christ—yeah, that's it really—thank Christ; because if He hadn't 'ave turned up I wouldn't be talkin' to you now.

Chapter 27

EDWIN

Religion, the spur on which many a war has been started, often shapes our lives and the lives of those we love. Edwin chose to share his story to illustrate that religion, however you choose to view it, is about faith, compassion and love; not control, not manipulation—nothing but love. His message is for those who choose to use religion as a stick with which to beat others, instead of a stick to help them stand.

It's true what they say you know, absence does make the heart grow fonder. I've been loving and missing my wife for 40 years. We're both dead, but we're in different places. She had some odd ideas you see. She could be difficult, loving her was not easy, but well, I was used to her. She *was* my wife, so duty being duty, I stood by her, even when she was wrong which, looking back, was most of the time.

She was a very difficult woman, what others would call spiteful. She took pleasure in another's pain. That, I couldn't understand, and often berated her for. She used to rail at me: tell me they were obviously being punished by God for some transgression. Very religious woman my Ingrid, *very*. I believe it was the fault of her upbringing. She only escaped her parents to marry me because I was of the clergy. I suppose I was considered a catch, though I didn't have hardly a penny to my name, and that remained a fact throughout our marriage. But my wife was a good manager, there was always food on the table, a*lways*. Might not have been much but we were grateful. We lived in a lovely house courtesy of the church, and I had my work, varied and often mundane though it was. I enjoyed my life—being needed, being useful—and I derived great pleasure, and even great inner peace from my faith.

My wife, poor soul, did not. She was constantly tormented by the need to make life difficult for others: interpreting the Bible's teachings to extremes . . . castigating parishioners, remonstrating with people too harshly. Often I had to undo her words and deeds without her knowing; life was lived on a knife edge. She considered me weak for not following her lead and never failed to point out my failings to me.

It was not all bleakness, there were times when we were happy. We would have quite stimulating conversations about life after death, about our Lord, but she was very rigid in her views. I soon realised that to challenge them was folly: her strong views underpinned her whole existence. To challenge that, to attempt to tear it down, would bring about total emotional and mental collapse for her.

As I neared retirement, my wife became increasingly difficult. I believe now that she was entering her blackest depression: she had depressions throughout our time together but would not seek help from doctors. She would ask only that I pray for her; I gave up trying to tell her that there are some ailments that need a little more than prayer. She completely lost her temper on one occasion that I put this to her, to the extent that there was a dent in the plaster wall of our dining-room for the remaining years we lived there caused by a pewter plate she sent spinning in my direction. She would lie on the couch with her head in my lap; I would sit with one hand on her forehead, and pray for healing for her. I believe this made some difference if she allowed it, for sadly, I see now that my wife was in control of how depressed she felt. She needed to control every aspect of her life and mine.

She passed with a stroke at a quarter past midnight. I was with her, beside her, sleeping fitfully when I heard a noise. I cannot even recall what sort of noise it was but something alerted me that all was not well with Ingrid. She was not breathing, still very warm and her eyes had a surprised look, taken unawares. It was very obvious that she had departed from life totally. I called our local doctor who had been a good friend and he came at once. The funeral was arranged: I thought to do this myself, but instead, approached a colleague who was more than happy to carry this out. I'm afraid my wife was not very well liked, so attendance at her funeral was poor. I was aware that the parishioners who did attend were there in support of me, for which I was very grateful. I decided not to retire after all. I still had work to do in the parish, fences to mend. I threw myself back into my work and found I enjoyed it more for my wife's lack of interference, much as it pains me to admit; but this has to be a truthful account.

I passed away myself, in the same bed, some five years later. I was not in the slightest bit afraid. I woke during the night. I remember thinking it would be light soon, so I estimated the time to be around 5 am. I was only half awake, if truth be told, and I did feel very odd. I experienced a fluttery feeling around my heart, something I had been having rather a lot of lately. I knew my heart was likely to give out sooner or later—hearts in my family had a nasty habit of collapsing on us, both my father and mother passed this way. I lay there in my bed in the half light and thought of them. I said aloud a prayer to our Lord that if he was to take me then, I was ready. I just knew with absolute clarity that my time had come. I was going home.

A figure appeared in my room, a semi-transparent figure. I felt such love, such overwhelming all-encompassing love that I wanted to cry like a child. I knew this person to be a messenger from the Lord. This was not an angel, not an angel as depicted in literature or art, but a messenger nonetheless. I closed my eyes and opened them again, testing my mind should I be seeing things, but he was still there, smiling at me. At once I became aware that he knew my thoughts as clearly as if I'd spoken them. He held out a hand to me; I knew if I took it I would pass into a spiritual existence. I took it willingly. His hand was warm and firm to the touch—I don't know that I expected otherwise. I felt myself to be moving at great speed but knew no fear. There is nothing to fear in passing from the physical to the spiritual. All that is you remains as you. The loss of physical body is no hardship, it is a release, a joyous, joyous release.

I met with everyone I had ever loved, liked and been a friend of, but I did not meet my wife. I was very puzzled by this and asked why it was so. I was immediately taken to see her and what a wretched condition she was in, as bitter and difficult as I remembered. She recognised me but instead of being pleased at my arrival, she berated me for her condition. I was most upset and tried to tell her she was making this existence difficult for herself. She was so unyielding in her belief that she was right, that her thoughts had created this wilderness she lived in. Her hatred of others, her manipulations, her bitterness had brought about the conditions in which she now lived. Her harsh religious views had no home in the spiritual worlds so she had to have a home for them for herself.

She had company! Many, many people were with her, doing penance of their own making, convinced that this was the spiritual world, the right spiritual world . . . how blind they are. I found this very distressing and asked what I could do to help. All I could do was continue to visit her and talk to her until she comes around of her own accord. These people have to want change, have to believe there is a better level of existence. It's a very long and hard road for some—of which my dear wife is one—but I continue to try.

So my message to you, dear people, is ease up on yourselves and others . . . ease up on your need to be right all the time. It does not serve you well in your life or this one. Instead allow your mind to be open, to be loving, even in the most trying of circumstances. Then, and only then, will you pass into a peaceful state of mind when you arrive here. Bitterness, anger, hatred and spite are ugly emotions . . . they have no place here, and their very presence in your thoughts corrode the goodness that is trying to prevail.

Please don't think I am preaching, I know this as a truth and I pass this onto you, so you too, with practise, will know it as a truth, and your non earthly life will be all the happier for it. Thank you for listening to me: it has been a pleasure to spend this little time with you.

CHAPTER 28

SONIA

This lovely, funny lady came to me one evening as I was winding down after a busy day. I was happy to listen, as I always am, I figure it would be rude not to when these people make such an effort to be heard. Sonia speaks to every woman who is in a relationship that doesn't make them happy. To every woman or man, who in their anxiousness to please another, isn't being true to 'themselves'.

My Alan was a lovely chap but he had funny habits. He couldn't kiss very well either, which was a nuisance, he was always wet. I liked a nice kisser, not one that had more spit than a camel.

He wasn't much of a provider either; he tried, but he kept losing his job. Every Friday for years I was in a state of panic at not being able to pay the rent, and wondering if he really was playing darts four nights a week. I was too afraid to ask in case he hit me. I was a walking advert for Prozac or a nervous breakdown.

I never knew if Alan was entirely faithful—his brother was very open to everyone except his wife that he had affairs. I met one of his girlfriends once—Christ alive you could have put a bridle on her. She told me he was going to leave his wife for her. When I got my breath back I told her he tells them all that, poor bugger, up until then she had thought she was the only one.

That's something I have never figured out—why do men have affairs with women uglier than their wife? I put this to Alan once, he looked uncomfortable for a minute, (which should have worried me), then said it's probably because they're grateful, and will do dirty stuff their wife wouldn't.

"What dirty stuff?" I said, still not as alert as I should have been.

"Oh I dunno," he said, "you know, dress up and stuff"

"What, like sexy underwear?" I said.

"Yes!" he said and changed the subject. The following week he bought me one of those sexy all-in-one things that were all the rage and did up between the legs. I tried it on but couldn't stand upright in it, I looked like Quasimodo. That went in the bin, and later on I found out he was having a fling with a woman the size of our shed; I knew this because I found a pair of her knickers in the car.

"Going camping?" I asked him holding them up—honest to God you could have got me and the kids in them. Of course, there was a scene—he accused me of not trusting him? Not trusting him! Can you believe it? I was such a fool, a trusting, gullible fool. After he lamped me for not trusting him, I went to my grandmother in tears.

After listening to me and providing enough tissues to mop up a small pond, she asked me if I loved him. I remember looking at her in surprise and realised with a sudden pin-sharp clarity that I didn't. I was in love with an idea of what love was like; I was in love with the idea of a happy marriage, two children, the picket fence. I had been in love with the whole nine yards, but in reality, as my gran pointed out, it wasn't real.

"That reality only existed in old films. Marriage was hard work and compromise, and most people don't do that very well because they marry too young and don't even know who they are, let alone who the person they have married is," she said. People either grew together or grew apart, and if they didn't grow together resentment would kill a marriage stone dead.

She said, "Yours died about three women and two black eyes ago!"

Now I had to decide whether to put up with it and have an unhappy life or leave and work my way back to a happier one. I left. I knew I wasn't someone who could live with other women in the marriage. He begged, he pleaded but I felt nothing, nothing at all.

The moment I decided to leave all the angst and worry and fear left me. I knew then I was making the right decision and this feeling, this gut feeling everyone talks about has served me well.

I struggled, of course I did, and there were moments of deep loneliness, but I learnt an awful lot about myself, and my children thrived because they weren't living in an atmosphere of simmering resentment and their mother's fear.

That's what I want to say to you girls and you chaps—too many people are not *living*. You are here for such a short time, and many of you are existing in situations where you feel you can't, or are too scared to get out of. It's such a waste, such a waste. No-one has control over you, and if you're in an abusive relationship definitely *get the heck out*. There is no excuse for hitting another person; men who do that and women too, there's something wrong in there. They're wired up wrong somewhere—that's all about fear and power, not love. Someone who *really* loved you would never want to hit you. No matter what they say, no matter how much they make you feel you deserved it—that's a laugh that is, deserved it? What a load of shit that is. Trouble is if you let these things continue, these situations, they get worse. Oh, they beg and cry afterwards, 'they didn't mean it', 'forgive me baby', 'you drove me to it because I love you so much'. It's all a lie, a big fat juicy lie. Then when you do forgive them *again* it's all rosy but within days they resent you for them looking weak, and it starts all over again. You can't win.

Remember this from one who has been there—no-one has control over you, no-one. They just want you to think they do; it's not real. Sooner or later, and hopefully before one of these people put you in a grave, you have to wake up to the fact that they only have as much power as you give them, so don't give them any. You can't help some people, and you certainly can't change people—stop thinking like that—it's pitiful the amount of women who think they can change their man.

I remember my mother in law telling me on my wedding day that I would have to accept that my husband would be unfaithful. I told her I wouldn't accept that. Looking back I probably knew for a while, and with small children I tried to hold it back, but living in fear as opposed to living free? In the end there was no contest.

Oh he got funny with me—I had court cases to go through. I had threats galore but I stood strong against it all. Many, many, times I was afraid, but never as afraid as I was living with him. All the struggle was worth it, because he eventually gave up and turned his attention to someone else. They always give up in the end, because they are cowards at heart.

Anyone who abuses, manipulates or intimidates has a big problem with their own insecurity, so takes out their inadequacies on other people; because inside, deep inside they *know* you are stronger than they are. They just don't want you to know that. Remember that, remember that because that strength, that inner strength and your gut instinct, that will save your life in more ways than you can imagine.

Don't let your death-bed thoughts be littered with regret, with all the things you should have done differently. Your death-bed thoughts should be like mine: peaceful, knowing you had done the best for your children, that you'd turned them out into the world knowing they were lovely, loving, stable people, knowing the value of themselves and others.

I think that's all I want to say to you, that is my reason for coming through—too many beautiful souls living in torment and fear, we see it all, everything. All the time, there are those of us trying to reach you, trying to reach you through your instinct, saying run, *run* while you still can. There is a better life waiting for you. Believe it.

Chapter 29

EVAN

A proud Welshman came through to me in a reflective mood, obviously still in awe of his experience and excited to make contact with someone still here; he wanted to reach out to allay fears and asked that I use his story. It is a pleasure to do so.

I died in a pit disaster: I didn't know what hit me really. It went all dark like, and I realised I was dead. The roof caved in, just like that it did, I didn't know nothin' about it. Black as yer hat it was. Funny thing about it was I always thought I'd go that way. I knew the pit would be the death of me.

Some days I could hardly get up the strength to go down there— hard to get me breath some mornings. Cough, cough, cough—I'd be, bringing up yards of filth from me lungs. I used to get it out of me system of a morning and try not to think about it for the rest of the day. I thought I had the cancer you know. Brutal it was, the pain in me lungs. I wasn't the only one, mind, not by a long chalk—we was always coughing and hacking. Mind you, we weren't miserable with it. I mean, what's the point in that? We had jobs to do and families to feed so we just got on with it—all you can do really.

I remember the morning I died as if it were yesterday. Time is nothing here you know, it's not measured out by the hour or the year. It was an ordinary kind of morning; the usual coughing up into the sink then making sure I'd swilled it away so as not to worry the wife. I'd been noticing bits of blood in it for a while but decided to ignore it, worrying didn't make it better. That's what made me fear I had the cancer, the muck and blood and brutal pain. I put it out of my mind and concentrated on getting to work. I met some lads on the way, we grunted our "Mornin's" to each other and stamped our way through the mist to the pit. That day had an eerie feel to it for me. I don't know if others felt it, I didn't ask, but I noticed they were a lot quieter going down than usual.

We had been working for a while when I thought I heard a noise. We always listened for noises down there, straining to understand what was happening in the earth. I heard what sounded like a muffled crack. A shout went up to get out, but there was no time, no time whatsoever. It was over very quickly, seconds really, for me at any rate—I was buried. Strangely, I wasn't afraid; there wasn't time.

I found myself outside the mine. I thought, "How did I get out here?" and in those few seconds it dawned on me I'd died.

No-one could see me. There was pandemonium out there. Then I saw the other men coming towards me, the other men I'd been with; they were looking as puzzled as I was. Then I realised our old foreman was behind them.

"Coming through lads," he said, pushing through them, "coming through."

Now, our foreman had died two years since but here he was, large as life. He called us all together and told us what had happened, that we had died. Some were so surprised they had trouble taking it in—we all did one way and another, I mean, we looked solid enough.

"Right lads," he said, "you've to come with me now. I'm going to look after you. Nothing to be afraid of. Right then, just relax and off we go." That was all he said, and here we are. I don't remember travelling—I don't recall moving away from the pit but we must have because next thing I know I'm seeing a couple of old mates of mine from the old days, some relations, and let me tell you the best of all, the three children me and the wife had lost years ago.

"The Lord's taken them," she said to me, "so one day we'll see them again." She was right. Oh, I wanted to tell her how right she was. She came up some years after me and I was waiting—we all were.

CHAPTER 30

MAL

This rather annoyed man came through one afternoon, apologised for bothering me, told me he would be quick and could I do it now? I was happy to oblige because it was clear he wasn't going to hang about!

I only went to the grocery store, that was all, just the grocery store. I was shot crossing the street. Caught in the cross fire of somebody else's fight. I've met the man since—the one who shot me. He was full of sorrys but I was still mad at him, I didn't want to die. I had a whole lot more living to do and he took that away, he had no right to do that. No-one has a right to do that. I wasn't about to forgive him anytime soon, no sir.

I was real mad for a long time, a long time. I was mad at my wife for wanting her groceries right then. I was mad at people getting in the way, but most of all I was mad at myself for not noticing something was going down. I trained all my working life for that kinda stuff. I was a police officer, for Christ sakes. Where was my training? I'd got sloppy, I sure am mad at myself for that.

I died right there in the street. Clean shot through the head, like I seen a hundred times in my career. I always thought some asshole would shoot me one day, but I thought as least I would die in the line of duty—you know, hopefully being a hero or something, not for a bag of goddamned groceries. How dumb is that? I guess I'm still mad about that. It's been a long time now, I try not to hold grudges; but I didn't get to see the things I had planned. I didn't get to see my grandkids grow. I didn't get to *have* any grandkids—what am I talking about?

I arrived here in an all time hurry—one second I was crossing the street, the next I wound up here. I remember feelin kinda strange, I remember movement but not a lot of anything else. I woke up here—it's a whole different place to where you are. This is living! Boy are you dead compared to us—there are no limitations here. I can do whatever the hell I want. I've seen old buddies, I've seen old criminal associates too—those that worked their way up, that is.

You gotta work at getting here, it ain't an automatic right. I was gratified to see that—I think the bad guys need to know they've been bad, they need to *feel* it, if they don't feel the result of their actions how can they know how wrong it was?

I didn't accept my death for a long time—still not sure I've come to terms with it. I know I have to let go of the anger, the injustice of it all, but it's hard. But I'm ok with that; I'm not ready to progress anyhow. I like it here—everyone I know is here or was here and I'm getting better at dealing with myself. I can see that holding onto anger only affects me.

The guy who shot me, he's moved on. He tried to help me, but I told him I didn't need his kinda help, he didn't try again.

I'm told I can't be angry forever, but I ain't done bad so far—it's been fifty three years! You'd think I'd be about ready to stop now, wouldn't you? I gotta keep working at it; I want peace of mind.

My wife is here, she loses patience with me, she says I was always mad at something, so nothing changes as far as she can tell. I told her it doesn't unless you want it to—guess I don't want change badly enough. I just can't seem to get past the feeling of being cheated out of my life, but like I said, I'm working at it. Be seein' you.

Chapter 31

Billy

Billy was a real 'jack the lad' type, talking to me in a London accent. A funny man, he thought coming through to say his bit would help to redeem him a bit more, I was happy to help out.

'Course, I didn't see it comin'—if I had I'd 'ave jumped out the way!

We hear them you know, the conversations that take place after we've died. Not *every* conversation—just the interesting ones. I got to hear what was said at my funeral. I heard my eldest daughter rebuke the youngest for smoking outside the crematorium. The youngest made an angry retort and told her sister where to get off. They never were close. My son was discussing the sale of my car to his uncle, my brother—who, incidentally, is tight as a tick and wanted the car for next to nothing. My son . . . son of his father, was sticking to his price, which I, and his uncle, knew was fair. They shook on the deal just as my coffin hovered into view.

The wife didn't show, well, ex-wife. Couldn't blame her really after the life we had and the divorce, but I thought maybe, just maybe, she'd show up out of respect. Turns out she'd gone to Spain. Didn't want to go to the funeral apparently—too many faces from the past; said she saw enough of them when she had to, and as she don't have to now, she ain't going. I saw her point, I did kind of throw her in the deep end when we was together. She didn't like some of my friends, come to think of it, she didn't like any of my friends.

"They ain't friends, Billy" she used to say, "they ain't friends—everyone of 'em would stab you in the back soon as look at you.

They're only here 'cause half of them's afraid of you and the other half will be."

I didn't listen, did I? Too busy being cock of the walk. Maybe, looking back I was just a cock. Thinking I was so important and all. Anyhow the wife, ex-wife, decides she'd light a candle for me out there in Spain apparently, and to my surprise . . . she did. Not in a church, on her patio. At the appointed hour of my funeral, or near as damn it, she lit a candle and put it on the patio. She sat there in front of it smoking a fag and thinking of what a bastard I'd been.

When she'd smoked the fag she put the candle out and said out loud, "Well, Billy old son. I don't know who's got you—God or the Devil—but wherever you are, I hope you're happy. Cause even though you gave me shit most of the time I really loved you, you maggot". Then she screwed the fag end into the patio with her shoe and went in search of more wine. She was never big on sentiment. Still had the shoes though I noticed—nearly had to get a fuckin' mortgage for those shoes, the receipt nearly gave me a heart attack. Still, she earned them putting up with me, not that I needed her to point it out, but she did anyway, several times as I recall.

I heard the conversations at the wake in the pub. It was a blessing, they said. Didn't see it coming, they said, I ask you! 'Course I didn't see it coming. Christ alive knows, I wasn't a fast mover, I mean with two gammy knees you're not going to be. But who the hell walks round looking skyward anyway? I still don't know what actually hit me, but whatever it was, it fell off a roof or off scaffolding or something. One minute I was walking along the pavement, the next I was up 'ere. I mean, it's all right, everyone's nice enough, but I wasn't expected—there was a hastily assembled reception committee. My nan was there and her sister, Aunt Maud—I used to think she was a witch when I was a kid (so many cats) I was surprised to see her up here. My nan, ever the soul of discretion, comes right to the point.

"You've died Billy," she says. "No point putting a gloss on it. You're a bit early but we can fit you in."

"Thank Christ for that," I thought. "Where would I go otherwise?" I remember being a bit shaken up by it all. I looked the same, everyone I met that I'd known in life looked the same.

Nan said "What did you expect?" She said just because you died didn't mean you got any nicer or got wings. I thought that was a bit pointed.

I settled in fairly quickly. Apparently you can work on yourself to become a better person than you were when you lived an earthly life. I'm looking into it, though with me it will be a long job, which is okay. I'm in no rush to face some things about myself; although I've overheard some shocking tales about things I'm s'posed to have done—heard all this from conversations among the living. My reputation is a bloody sight worse now I'm dead than it was when I was alive, and it was bad enough then.

Course, I've met some of the lads here, ones I helped on their way if you know what I mean. They don't hold no grudges, which is just as well 'cause there's no escaping here—no one to bump off 'cause they've offended you, na, you gotta sort it out. That takes some doing I can tell you. Some of them couldn't string two words together when they were alive and some of them still make fuck all sense to me, but I'm working at it; when I've a mind to that is.

I keep popping in on the family, making sure they're alright. Trying to guide them a bit you know. The ex has a new fella, seems decent enough; but if he lays a hand on her he'll find the fucking wardrobe falling on him in the middle of the night. Old habits die hard and all that, ain't that the fuckin' truth.

Most of the time I work with young thugs and old crims who come over unexpectedly or who bring themselves. It's a worthwhile job; only job I ever had that didn't pay big money. That's something I've learned since bein' 'ere—money means jack shit. It's useful in life of course, gets you by, but what really counts, what earns you the brownie points up 'ere is what you do for other people outta the goodness of your heart 'cause you want to, not because there's something in it or you can rob some poor bugger blind. No, it's only the good that counts.

It was painful at first for me, seeing the lost opportunities when I could've helped someone out and chose not to. Selfish bastard I was then—not now though. Redeemed I am, well, partly. Like I said, there's still some areas of my murky past that I want to remain murky. Embarrassed and ashamed of it I am, but I'll turn to that page when I'm ready. In the meantime I'm doin' all the good I can; makin' up for lost time you might say. Be seein' ya, ta ra!

CHAPTER 32

ADAM

Adam was one of the first people coming through to me, a powerful personality just wanting to share his experiences. He wasn't sure many people would want to listen because the men of war often, those of preceding generations, become forgotten men, just numbers. I assured him his story was so powerful that I was sure others would want to hear it. Oh well, if you say so, was his reply, they tell me you know what you're doing so here goes . . . .

A single bullet. That's all it was, a single bullet. Got me right in the middle of the forehead. A bulls-eye in any other game! They didn't find me for three weeks. I was a bloody mess by then—the constant rain and the shelling. There were other bodies all around me, on top of me and all around—bits of bodies most of them. I knew a bullet was going to get me. Well, I didn't know it would be a bullet for sure, I just knew I wasn't going to be coming home. Lots of us knew it. I can't describe the feeling, it was just a knowing.

I wasn't sure whether I believed in God before I went to war. My mother did; I told her she prayed enough for both of us. She told me not to take the Lord's name in vain because, odds on, I'd call on him one day and I'd want him to be listening. She was right too. In those filthy trenches, in those godforsaken conditions, the lives of hundreds of men being snuffed out in a second, oh, I prayed alright. We all did, one way or another. Some of us raged at God, blaming him. I used to think there wasn't a lot of point in that; it wasn't God that started the war. Men start the wars, God has to do the mopping up.

When my mate Alfred was hit—blown up he was—I saw it. He was there as solid as you like and then he was gone, like vapour but full of little bits of Alfred. Two other blokes went with him but I barely knew them. I couldn't believe it, I was in shock for days, not that I got any help with it. You just got on with it, with the fighting. When the shock wore off, anger set in, hate really. I used to think even five Germans weren't worth the air Alfred breathed. I'd kill without compunction.

I must've killed any amount of Germans before one got me. He must have been a crack shot because I'd only stuck my head up over the trench no more than a couple of inches, then Bang! That was it, blotto. The bullet knocked me on my arse. I didn't feel it, which was a blessing.

I didn't know I was dead at first. I was surprised, but at the same time, not so surprised to see Alfred making his way down the trench. He saluted me and I thought, "Dozy bugger, what's he saluting me for? We're the same rank." He laughed like he'd heard me. He did hear me but I knew I'd only thought it. He touched my arm and I grabbed him. I couldn't believe he was whole, solid, real.

"But you were killed!" I said.

"I know," he said. "Are you coming with me?"

"Where to?" I asked.

"Freedom," he replied, "just over there." He pointed away from the battle.

"I can't leave," I said.

"Yes you can. You have to," he replied. "Look." He turned me round to see me sitting in the trench.

"Bloody hell, that's me."

"Yes," he laughed. "You're dead too."

"I am?" I said. I tell you I was stunned. I went over to where I was sat and had a closer look.

"Well, blow me," I thought, "I'm bloody well dead. Well, at least the Jerry was a decent shot."

Alfred said, "Come on, we have to go. I've others to get as well."

Others? I looked around and men were leaving their bodies everywhere I looked. Some were laughing! Imagine that, laughing. Some looked very low but others were encouraging them. We all headed off in the same direction. I turned to look back once more. All I saw was mess, carnage and mess; then I realised there wasn't a man alive back there, not a single one. What a waste, I thought, Alfred turned to me and said not to dwell on that now; it was over for us, we were free. He said we had to get a move on, there were plenty more chaps to collect, God help them.

Some chaps were most put out to find they were dead. Some caused no end of trouble, demanding to go back, and all that kind of nonsense. I could understand it—they had wives and families. I didn't have a sweetheart waiting for me, just my parents; I knew they'd be heartbroken and that worried me. I got to see them several times: because I'd settled in so easily and had accepted my fate I was able to visit them.

I was there when they got the telegram. My mother wouldn't open it; she knew, she just didn't want it confirmed. The telegram sat on the mantelpiece for three days; Father opened it in the end, he couldn't stand the not knowing for sure. They never got over my death; learnt to live with it, but never got over it.

I was there when they passed, within three weeks of each other. Father had a stroke, and Mother, well Mother just gave up, her heart just stopped. She'd been asking God to take her every day since Father died, I'd been gone 30 years by then.

Father saw me come for him, I was stood right at the end of his bed. He spoke my name before he died; it was the first word he'd managed since his stroke a fortnight before.

He said "Adam," and tried to lift his arm.

Mother looked right where I was standing, but I know she didn't see me; she cried, she knew.

I took Father that night: he was as pleased as punch, and said, "But what about Mother?"

I said to be still, that she was coming soon. I was there to collect my Mother too.

"I knew you'd come," she said. I can't begin to describe how happy she was. She was found in her bed by her sister, who said to the doctor it was the first time she'd seen Mother smile in thirty years.

CHAPTER 33

JULIE

Julie is another equally lovely child, more worldly wise than Karis, but wanting to share some nuggets of wisdom from her hilarious grandmother in whose keeping she is, until her parents meet up with her.

I thought I'd tell you what it's like, being what you call 'dead'. Funny really, 'cause we are more alive than you are; we can see everything you know, everything—even the stuff you don't want us to! We can't come and visit all the time of course, we have things to do too. I mean, getting used to where we are takes a while, some people don't settle in very well at all, always moanin' that they want to go home. I can understand it, I mean it is a bit odd at first, like being plonked in a foreign country. Everyone speaks the same language which is a help, but you don't know your way around when everyone else seems to—a bit like your first day at senior school, only without the death grip on your bowels.

I saw my angel not long after I arrived, I had to look twice before I believed it myself, he looked distracted, as if he was in a hurry and a bit worried. I said this to my Nan who was with me, she looked at him as he swept past and said, "Oh he would, he's one of the angels who's responsible for helping people do stuff."

I said, "What, you mean he's got two jobs?" I was surprised at this because Mum always said that everyone had their own angel, so I didn't understand why I had to share mine.

Nan said angels had to multi-task because they couldn't sit around waiting for someone like me to do something interesting, not when half my life had been spent watching telly.

"I mean," she said, "even an angel could only stomach so much of daytime television before they went off their head." Apparently angels need a diet of light and goodness and you don't get much of that on television these days. Nan said that our lives weren't interesting enough for our angels to hang around every minute of the day.

"Besides," she said, "they liked their own company and just checked on us from time to time."

She described it like everyone on Earth is in a playpen, every now and then your angel would check on you and if you looked as though you were about to climb the side of the playpen and do something rash they would all nudge each other and watch you make a hash of it. Some would slap their foreheads and wonder at the wisdom of humanity; some would try to console your angel, knowing all the time that he'd got landed with a half-wit and would be grateful it wasn't them; and the others would nod in silent agreement and take bets on how you were going to get out of this one. Meanwhile you'd be floundering about in a mire of your own making, wondering if you ever had a guardian angel and if so, where the hell was he?

"What you fail to realise . . ." Nan said, cocking her head and looking me right in the eye to emphasise the seriousness of her words—she used to do this when she wanted to get an important point across, like trying to find the person who dared to pinch the last strawberry cream from the Quality Street, Nan loved strawberry creams with a passion, Granddad used to say that it was a passion matched only by her intolerance of organised religion and magnolia paint—Nan stared right in my eyes and said, "What people fail to realise is that they have to ask their angel for help."

She said the angels can't step in willy-nilly; as people we have free will, so if we want to muck our lives up we can get right on and do it, and there are those who seemed hell bent on making a career of it. If people stopped to think for a minute, and asked the universe for direction it would come. Not, she said, in a bolt of lightning; the answers will come in your thoughts or through your intuition.

Angels can also organise it for you to meet someone who can help you, they give you messages in dreams, to help you help yourselves. They can give messages to psychic people, but they can't turn up in person very often, because it's just too far to come and their wings get tired.

I said, "Couldn't they carry a packed lunch, like we did if we went on a long journey?"

Nan says no, like she'd said, angels feed on a diet of light and goodness, and that's in short supply in some of the places they are asked to go, so they have to conserve their energy for the big jobs, not waste it helping people with their maths homework or finding their car keys. She said if you do ask for help with maths homework, that message is passed down the line to someone who was good at maths when they were alive and still wants to keep their hand in—makes sense, don't you think?

She said, "After all, who said angels were any good at maths? When you need a plumber you don't call an electrician do you? Beats me why people don't think of this for themselves—I mean what makes people think angels are good at everything? No, they delegate; they know there are loads of spirit people scanning the heavenly message boards for someone in need of their talents.

Nan looked at my face. "Oh yes there are," she said. "Think about it . . . if someone like a artist spent all their life honing their craft, they're hardly going to want to stop doing it just because they died. That would be a waste! No, they busy themselves here, but when a message comes in that someone in the physical world has asked for help from an artist, they fall over themselves in the rush to see who is best qualified to help. Then they set about trying to inspire the tortured artist with fresh ideas; the person who asked for help feels the inspiration and the work pours forth."

"Some," she added, "even remember to send up thanks, which always goes down well over here, no-one likes to think they are taken for granted, even if they are dead. But," she said, "people should be sure they really want what they ask for."

Nan had a point. I remember hearing Mum saying a prayer years ago. She asked the angels to help her catch my dad—she was sure he was seeing someone else and it was drivin' her mad. They must have been listening, because a week later she caught my dad snuggling up to her friend, Margery Collins, in the garage; Margery said Dad was just checking her spark plugs.

Mum yelled, "Well you would call them that you, tit-less wonder!" and threw a monkey wrench at her and Dad. He ducked, and the wrench hit the car smashing the windscreen, and then Mum threw everything within reach at the pair of them. The car was full of dents—Dad and Margery had to duck out of the garage and run for it! Mum couldn't stop laughing, in fact she laughed till she cried, and she cried a lot.

Nan said that's something else we learn in heaven, forgiveness. This doesn't come easy to some, and to others not at all. Nan says it's no good carrying bitterness around with us, all it does is eat us up and make us ill. The other person is walking around enjoying their life, completely unaffected, so what's the point? Then when you get up here you have to work through it—see what your part was and why things happened the way they did. Nan says we could save ourselves all of that by sorting it out while we're still alive. She say's by being mad at someone for a long time you are giving your power away to them, and why would you want to do that?

"Anyway," Nan said, "People always get their comeuppance; granted, sometimes it's difficult to wait long enough to see it, but sooner or later it happens. This 'what comes around, goes around' stuff that everyone talks about is true. But instead of taking brake fluid to an ex-boyfriends car, you can ask your angel to help you to deal with the pain of betrayal, because it's too painful a load for you to carry. Of course, this option is not always as satisfying as watching your faithless ex sobbing all over the melted remains of his Nissan Micra, but at least ensures that you don't chalk up karma of your own."

Nan said that the very best revenge is to get on with your life—get your hair done, put it around that you have a new and adventurous, younger, fitter lover with more hair on his head, and save your sobbing and self-pity for when you are alone. Ask your angel to help you. Angels have extra strength for helping people with emotional stuff like that, and if it gets a bit much for even them, they can call on St Jude for advice.

I asked Nan who Saint Jude was, "Patron Saint of Lost Causes," she said. "She's a dab hand at dealing with all kinds of people problems—its bread and butter stuff to her. She hates magnolia paint too; she says if people had more colour in their lives they'd be a lot less miserable."

Nan said that being dead is a lot easier than being alive. She said this way we live forever in the hearts of people who love us, and after a while they only remember the best bits about us instead of having us, around to remind them of our annoying habits. She's great my Nan. I missed her loads when she died, now I'm with her all the time, and I take notice of what she says. So I thought I'd tell you about her, because it might help someone to think differently about their life—you know, wake them up a bit. I can hear her calling me, got to go now. Bye then, bye.

Chapter 34

Edward

This proud gentleman came through to me one Sunday afternoon, he hoped he wasn't bothering me but would I like to hear his story? He reduced me to tears as I wrote, and even now, years later, every time I read his words I see his beaming blue eyes, his amazing smile, his Englishness, and I am privileged he chose me to share his story with.

It began quietly enough, hardly noticed really—the forgetfulness. The usual stuff we all do from time to time; you know, go to the fridge for something, open the door and promptly forget what it was you went there for. That used to happen to me all the time: I'd leave my glasses upstairs and forget where I left them, that sort of thing. But this, this was different; Faith was different.

Oh she was in there most of the time in the beginning, at least ninety per cent of the time I'd say; just the odd fridge incident back then. But sadly over the next three years I noticed that she tired very quickly, and was much more forgetful. We would laugh about it—I didn't want her to worry.

"After all," I'd tell her, "these things happen to us all with age." Sometimes I would catch her looking a little confused, distracted almost; of course I knew that she was leaving me even then, and my heart would give a little leap of fear.

I came in to the house one day after pottering in the garden to find my wife in the corner of the living room, facing the wall like a naughty child; crying she was, crying in the corner. I looked at her and wondered whatever was wrong. I called to her gently.

"Faith," I said, "Faith, are you alright Love?" She didn't answer me. I put my hand on her arm and she grabbed at me in fright.

"I'm afraid," she cried, "I'm afraid. I'm in the corner and I don't know how to get out." That broke my heart. I turned her around and sat her in her chair, gave her a squeeze and went to make us both a nice cup of tea. I felt a crushing sadness, and as I filled the sugar bowl I had a little cry at the realization that my wife was lost in her own living room. I knew then with absolute certainty that I was losing Faith.

Of course if I knew then what I know now, I'd have popped us both a couple of pills to see us safely off, but you don't think like that at the time. No, at the time you are trying to pretend it isn't happening, or maybe it's a one-off, her tablets not agreeing with her, anything but face the fact that your wife's mind is all muddled.

After a time, as her mental health deteriorated further, my darling wife, much to my distress, had to go into a nursing home. I scoured the locality for the one that I felt was the best one for her. I used to sit there with her every day and witness the confusion in her poor head, all those electrical messages misfiring.

Occasionally two wires would connect for a moment and Faith would come back to me . . . smile, squeeze my hand and the love would shine in her eyes for maybe just seconds, and then the wire would shake loose and she would look at me as though I were a stranger to her; or worse still she would think I was the doctor and begin unbuttoning her blouse. I would quickly try to do it up again; the last thing I wanted was people to think I was interfering with my wife. The nurses at the home were very good, they were used to this, and to my horror informed me that Faith thought every man who came into the nursing home was the doctor, and was regularly unbuttoning her blouse—it was then that I started buying her jumpers.

It was so dispiriting seeing her like that—losing my wife while she was still alive. How unspeakably cruel that she and I were now strangers to each other. I would lie in my bed in the early days and howl at the sheer injustice of it all. Why did I have to lose Faith? She had been a good and loving wife for sixty years.

Our lives seemed to have gone by in the blink of an eye; I had been eighty-seven last birthday. Years ago I can remember thinking eighty-seven sounded ancient, but I was as sprightly as I ever was, and still had all my own hair and most of my teeth.

I still visited Faith every day. She didn't know me at all by then—no glimpses of recognition, no long buried memory struggling to the surface, but I still sat with her, talked to her. She stared my way occasionally and occasionally gave a funny half-smile at something only she could see. I'd watch the nurses come and go, they did everything for her; they were very good but they didn't have time to sit with her, so I was there every day for the last eight years. I only missed a week when I was suddenly rushed into hospital myself with a heart attack, but I was soon out of there.

"I couldn't be anywhere else but with my wife," I said, that was the deal I made with God, you see. I could be with her, stay with her. I don't think she noticed I'd been away, and I had left instructions in my will that she wasn't to be told about my funeral.

I did the rounds of the other residents while I was visiting Faith—they didn't get many visitors and the only ones who spoke were those who were leaving this mortal coil. Some a little bewildered, I'd smile and tell them not to worry, everything will be fine. The rest of the time I just sat there with Faith. I heard the first piece of good news on a Tuesday, two nurses were talking.

"We are losing Faith." they said, checking her heart and pulse. Hooray! In life my Faith was my all, my everything, and now ... not long now.

"Not long now my precious girl," I whispered in her ear, "and angels will carry you on gossamer wings to me, I am waiting for you." I had been waiting a long, long time for my Faith to be restored to me. I stood at the end of her bed so that the first thing she would see after leaving her earthly life would be me. I wanted her to know that I had never left her, she passed during the night... and oh what a joyous moment that was.

Everything was quiet, there was just a night light giving the room a gentle glow, but I could have lit the whole room up with sheer excitement. She left her earthly body at precisely 2.32am—she rose from her bed and grinned at me with such a look of wonderment and surprise. We are together again, as much in love as we always were. She is all I ever wanted or needed, and I am blessed.

Please tell people who are losing a loved one to dementia that they will be returned to themselves on leaving an earthly life. Please don't berate yourselves for not visiting as often as others think you should. I had the time and the stamina, but I know others don't, and the emotional difficulty of carrying such a burden is harrowing and depressing.

People with dementia live in their own world, and in their own way they are often happy. Accepting that they are lost to you for a while is the only way to cope with such a cruel disease, but you will see them again in time—laughing and as loving as they always were. My Faith has been restored to me, and I can tell you this... my afterlife is glorious. Love really does conquer all.

Chapter 35

Dementia

These words were given to me in response to my question about dementia and how people can best deal with this terrible disease when it is affecting someone they love.

When someone you love has dementia the brain is not functioning properly, due to, in simplified terms, the brain cells misfiring and loose wires floating about. In its panic, because whoever was driving appears to have temporarily left, the mind is raiding the memory banks in no particular order, so what comes out can be confused, aggressive, provocative, rude, happy or sad. This can be due to information that has been stored for decades, from books they have read, films they've seen, situations they have witnessed and family memories.

It is unwise to correct the person or to tell them they're talking rubbish—what you must do is go along with the conversation, humour them; don't forget that by now they probably think you are the one being idiotic. 'What do you mean you can't see uncle Fred? He's stood there plain as day!' (you can be sure he is and is no doubt finding it all very amusing)

You see, I believe their spirit, the true essence of them, has partly excarnated (half way out of their physical body) and is in communication with their loved ones already in the spirit world. This is never more obvious than when your ailing relative is telling you they've seen their mother, father or sibling. They have truly done so, because the physical body is just a vehicle we move around in, it's not the real us, and the spirit of a dementia sufferer has decided it's had enough of trying to operate a faulty vehicle and has gone walk about instead.

Trying to rationalise with a dementia sufferer is like trying catch water in a sieve—frustrating, so don't do it. Relax and allow the person's train of thought to run out of steam or change track; it will do so with alarming regularity.

During some conversations you will notice that, at times, the dementia sufferer will gradually seem as though they are coming back to themselves, and can respond to you and to normal conversation. Be grateful for those moments because a few wires have reconnected—their spirit has responded to the emotional presence you are emanating, and has struggled to return to you for however long as they are able, whether that is seconds, minutes, hours or days.

It is ok to be sad at not being recognised by the person you love so much, but be sad in private not in front of them. If you leave them with sadness or tears, this memory will be added to their store and replayed, probably when you're not there, and you don't want them crying and not knowing why. As hard as it is for you, leave them with a smile knowing that the person you love is still in there somewhere and their spirit, the true essence of them, knows you love them.

When they eventually leave this life, the love you have for them will carry them safely into the arms of other people they have loved and lost before, and one day you will see them again as whole and as loving as they had once been and they will know of all you did for them in this life. And that my friends, is what a true and unselfish love is all about.

Chapter 36

Marnie

Marnie is a story given to me by her grandson. I felt it should be included because, apart from it being hilarious, there is a message for all of us here in not taking everyone at face value.

My gran used to tell me horror stories to get me to sleep. As I recall I would try to drop off before she got to a scary bit, so all in all they worked. I heard her talking to my mum once who was complaining about her story telling.

Gran said, "Well it didn't do you any harm!"

Mum said, "Didn't do me any harm—I'm forty-four years old and I still have to have the landing light on; and not only that, if the broom cupboard door is ajar at night I have to run past it. How normal is that?"

I can't remember hearing what my gran replied, but she kept on telling me scary stories. They'd start off ordinarily enough—you know, once upon a time, like normal stories—but Gran quickly got bored with the niceness of them. So Cinderella became a schizophrenic, knife-wielding maniac biding her time, and the ugly sisters were drug runners for the prince who was head of the local mafia. Cinders had to pretend to be all sweetness and light because she wanted to marry the prince for power and money, so she would invariably bump off her sisters in various and often ingenious ways. The prince was always as thick as shit and never saw any of this coming which baffled me—I thought you'd have to be able to spot a killer if you were in the mafia. Gran said if you used as many drugs as he did, you'd be thick as shit too 'cause they addled your brain and made your nose drop off.

Gran had a bit of a thing for the mafia. She'd been on a coach trip to Italy once years ago and swore she had dinner with the godfather. Apparently she got chatting to some grizzled old Italian, and next thing you know she's treating him to a margherita pizza and ribald tales of her youth. Whether he understood a word is debatable, although it got lively when she showed him the flick knife she always carried.

Don't get me wrong, my gran could be as lovely as anyone else's but there was this side to her that loved a drama. She said she lived on adrenaline once and now she had a taste for it. Waiting for pension day to join all the other coffin-dodgers in the post office didn't cut it for her; so if nothing was happening locally she'd go and stir something up.

I remember when I was having a few problems at school with bullying; I begged Mum not to tell Gran but turns out she'd overheard me anyway. She could've worked as a spy for the government, my gran. She could creep around anywhere.

I said this to her once and she said, "I did that for a while, but it wasn't for me, I can't toady up to people who are stuck up their own arse. Besides, half of them don't know what they're doing, and the other half are a shifty lot of bastards!"

I was coming out of school this particular day and the two bullies were behind me, callin' me names an threatening to do me over. I saw Gran at the gates and I knew from the look she gave me that she didn't want me to speak to her, so I started walking home with these two idiots behind me, and Gran behind them. Tell the truth I was more worried at what Gran was going to do to them, than what they were going to do to me.

When we turned into a quiet leafy street they started to push me around, and Gran snapped at them to leave me alone. One of them squared up to her and said, "What you gonna do about it Granma?" I almost felt sorry for him.

Gran drew herself up to her full four foot eleven and a half, opened her trusty flick knife and said "I'm going to have your balls for a purse young man!" The look of horror on his face more than made up for weeks of bullying I'd had. Then Gran tripped him with a neat ankle movement and he landed in an undignified heap on the pavement.

Gran looked at me and said in a loud voice, "You better get along home, young man." Meanwhile matey-boy was struggling to get to his feet and from the look on his face, as far away from Gran as possible. I needed no second telling, I was off.

I told mum as soon as I burst through the door. She looked at the calendar and said, "Thought so—full moon. She always gets a bit playful around a full moon." Funnily enough I never got bullied again. They never knew the old lady was my gran—she said she helped the bully to his feet, which seemed to frighten him more, and told him he was lucky it was Wednesday, because she normally carried her gun on Wednesdays, but as it was full moon she couldn't trust herself not to use it, so she carried her flick knife instead. She even showed him the little nicks in the blade where she'd hit bone in the past, but he didn't seem awfully keen on looking.

Mum said, "You didn't tell me you'd ever hit bone with it, you must be losing your touch Mother." Gran said it had probably been her arthritis throwing her aim off a bit even then.

I never knew whether to believe Gran or not, but when Mum joined in I was even more confused. I asked Mum if Gran had ever really killed people once. She said as far as she knew, it was more than once, and they had been asking for it.

She said, "Your granddad had been terrified of her at certain times of the month because her killer instinct was to the fore—he was always glad if she was on assignment then, and used to feel vaguely sorry for whoever she was hunting."

Gran slowed up a bit as she got older. She wasn't so good on her legs and her eyesight wasn't brilliant, but her hearing was phenomenal—she could always tell when I was coming down the path. I asked how she could tell, and she said it was through her days in Poland helping the partisans dispatch Germans. She had to be able to tell whether the twig snapped under a jackboot or a partisans shoe before she shot them. She said she could tell a jackboot a mile off, because most of them had an arsehole attached to them, and its well known that arseholes make a lot of noise!

I loved my gran. She made the best casserole and dumplings ever. She said she had to make a casserole once with half a rabbit, two tired carrots and a handful of potatoes—apparently this was in Poland, she was stuck in a cottage in the boondocks, which means the back of beyond to you and me. She said they lived off that casserole for a fortnight; and if she ever saw a rabbit again she'd shoot it from further away, so next time there'd be more of it left to cook.

As kids we used to laugh at Gran's stories—we knew she had probably been a bit wild in her youth, like we all are, but we never really believed her. I mean she was my *gran*.

When she died we had a quiet funeral, just the family and one or two friends of Gran's. They brought their own wreaths—one from Poland, one from Italy, and one from Russia.

Chapter 37

Existence

'Existence' was given to me one cold wintery day when I was idly wondering what it's like on the other side of life for those who haven't believed in anything.

We are not as we once were.

The part that was *us*, the true essence of *us*, remains the same. The physical body limits us in the physical world. That which is spirit, our spirituality—however we perceive it as individuals—lives on and can never die.

The transition from physical to spirit is not an easy one for some. Those who never believed in anything, other than what they could see or understand, are limited at first by their unwillingness to explore avenues of possibility.

All are warmly received, and gently, very gently, eased into realising of their own accord that theirs was not the only way to reach a spiritual existence. Some do not take it well, but all, in time, come to realise that there is only one God.

However you choose to name him, and whichever path you choose to reach him, he will be waiting.

CHAPTER 38

HEAVEN & HELL

'Heaven and Hell' is the answer I received when I asked what happens to child abusers and murderers, who think they have got away with their vile actions in this physical life. This should be enough to make even the most hardened abuser think twice. If not, the answer will bring some comfort to those who have lost innocence, trust and, in some cases their lives to perpetrators of evil acts.

I'll tell you what it was like for me. I was always told when I was a child, that Heaven and Hell were separate places. Well, I can tell you now, they're not. They are the same place, just separate areas, different sides of the same coin as it were—quite a surprise. Thankfully, not an unpleasant one for me, as I landed on the right side, heads you might say.

But for others, for others it must be a nightmare place. I can say that with some authority, because I've been to look. I shan't be going back, it's hellish, truly. But interestingly, it's a hell of their own making, and there appears to be differing levels of existence there. I found it difficult enough being at the level where some truly obnoxious people reside—perpetrators of evil against children, sadists, bullies, the lower end of the human food chain.

I thought it odd how these people thought they had done no wrong—how they continued to rationalise their actions, continued to hold fast to the entirely self-serving aspects of their characters. They were regularly contacted by higher beings, trying to help, but not getting very far. These people, this flotsam, didn't see they needed help. They were content to a point, but must have wondered where everyone else was; or maybe they continue to be so absorbed by their chosen lifestyle that they see no reason to change.

You see change, real change, in their conditions can only come about through introspection, by facing the parts of themselves that are unwholesome, and in so doing, in an honest and penitent way, they are released. But this is not an easy route, *not at all*, and a great number turn back, unable to progress through fear and shame. You see, they have to physically experience the fear and pain they caused the victims of their machinations, there is no escape from that.

It has to be a voluntary gesture; these people have to *want* change, but change for its own sake, not theirs. Selfish thoughts are heard and seen by the great and the good, there is no room for manoeuvre—no-one to be cheated or manipulated. Every dark, self-serving thought or action is seen immediately, and that person is returned to the level from which they came, sinking back into the morass that is a writhing mass of moral ineptitude.

Let them know that. Let all the people who may think their actions of this kind are not known about . . . let them know they walk through a different door when they pass this way.

PART II
My Life

Chapter 39

Over the years there have been a great many people whom I have helped: both those who are soon to pass from this world, and those who have lost loved ones. I could recount many, many stories of my own where mediumship combined with compassion and tolerance has made a difference to the lives of others, but there are a few specific examples that I would like to share with you—again, to aid your understanding of contact with what we know as the spirit world.

I have lost count of the calls I have had over the years to use my experiences to help people. I go to people's houses, houses they have feared to be haunted. I am able then to tell them that it's their mother or brother or father, a loved one who has passed who is wanting their attention—wanting to tell them everything will be alright, wanting to tell them that they know, in detail, of the issues that are causing worry, and as a result, I am able to put their mind at rest.

One house I was called to wasn't being 'haunted' by a family member—it was a former resident. Albert cared enough for the people living in his former home to make his presence felt in a very helpful way. It was 10.30pm when the frantic phone call came from Graham, who had been given my telephone number by a friend of a friend. He and his wife Diane were being scared witless by a ghost. Could I help?

Graham told me that they had both been woken in the night to 'feel' someone in their room. Lights kept being switched off, taps were turned off, doors were being closed, there were rushes of cold air, and light bulbs were exploding in their sockets. Most frightening of all, however, someone or something invisible had lain between them on their bed, and both Diane and Graham had seen the shadowy figure of a man walking around their flat.

My clairvoyance immediately came into play as I listened over the phone to Graham's catalogue of events and I was able to dispel his biggest fear; this wasn't malevolent poltergeist activity. I was able to tell them that the shadowy figure and rushes of cold air were, in fact, quite common in my experience. After again reassuring my frantic caller that there was most definitely not an evil presence in their home, I took their address and arranged to visit them the following evening. Then, before going to bed I shot up a prayer that the whole family would get some sleep that night.

I found myself the next evening in the North Devon seaside resort of Westward Ho! I followed the somewhat hazy directions, and after a third time around the one way system I finally found Graham and Diane's flat in the basement of an imposing Victorian building.

Graham and Diane met me at the door and proved to be a completely normal couple in their late twenties. Diane was obviously nervous and seemed reluctant to re-enter the flat unless Graham was glued to her side. Both were level headed people, not given to flights of fancy—Graham was a builder, and you don't get much more down to earth than a builder, Diane was a nurse.

As we entered the flat I became aware of a spirit presence. I said nothing for the time being, and sat in the lounge to hear what the family had been experiencing. Graham and Diane had been aware of a presence in the flat for about twelve months, but it hadn't bothered them previously because there had always been a nice atmosphere when it was about. In the last two weeks however, things had taken what they felt to be a menacing turn.

One night Diane had been woken in the early hours by a tightness of the bedcovers. Turning to Graham to berate him for lying against her, she discovered he was on the far side of the bed and then realised that someone or something invisible was laid against her. Overwhelming fear gripped her, but eventually she was able to find her voice and called for Graham to wake up. His first thought on waking was that Diane was lying tight up against him. Now fully awake they could both feel body heat from their visitor, and then saw three indentations in the duvet as whomever or whatever was there, climbed off. Exit a very frightened Graham, Diane and children to Graham's mothers for the remainder of the night.

Other recent happenings were minor in comparison: tapping noises, the guitar in the corner being strummed, light bulbs popping, doors being shut and taps being turned off when no-one was anywhere near them. Unable to stand the increasing strain, Graham had phoned various organisations, clairvoyants and churches up and down the West Country asking for help; only to be repeatedly told that they had an 'entity' which no-one felt qualified to deal with. They were even told, in one instance, to surround their eldest child's bed with candles. I was livid. Not one of these so-called professional bodies or individuals would help, and had now left Graham and Diane convinced they had a poltergeist in the flat. Diane said she felt she was going out of her mind with worry.

As I listened to them I became aware of a spirit gentleman who was haunting the flat. Everyone else felt his presence and went quiet; watching me intently as I silently communicated with him and then passed the information on to them.

His name, he said, was Albert Evans, and he had lived in the part of the house that was now Graham and Diane's flat. He had been a music teacher. He was a lonely man who had never had a family and had died there of a heart attack.

He said he enjoyed living with Graham and Diane's family—it was he who was switching off lights, turning off taps that had been left running by the children and closing doors, habits he had got into while living there to preserve the limited resources he had.

The entire conversation took place while Albert wandered around the room, his shadowy figure visible to everyone. He was terribly worried because Graham and Diane had talked of moving house after the bed incident: he didn't want this to happen and felt he was being blamed for what was the dog's fault!

At this point I explained to Graham and Diane that I had also been aware of another invisible guest in the flat—a large German shepherd dog called Sadie that had, my clairvoyance reliably informed me, belonged to Diane some years previously. Amazed, she confirmed that she had indeed once had a German shepherd called Sadie, who had died.

"Well that's who was on your bed that night," I said. Diane just stared at me wide-eyed as the feelings of recognition and relief flooded over her, and a load of worry and concern visibly lifted from her shoulders.

And the exploding light bulbs? "Not of my doing," said Albert. The electrics were such that anything over a 40 watt bulb just blew. Keep to that low wattage and all would be fine.

The atmosphere in the room had changed dramatically. "Well," said Diane, "that's alright then. We'll stay now and Albert can keep conserving heat and light all he wants!" I was very pleased as I left to have been able to help the family and Albert to understand each other.

I visited the flat the next week to see how everyone was getting on. Albert was still doing his nocturnal wanderings, looking in on the children as they slept, still shutting doors. He saw it as his job to keep the family safe, and Graham and Diane were quite happy about that.

Diane was still a bit nervous when she met Albert on the landing one night soon after I visited so she now speaks to Albert before she leaves the bedroom, asking him to make himself scarce when she has to visit the bathroom in the middle of the night.

Graham regularly talks to Albert, and once had to tell him off when the television, controlled by remote, kept turning over to a cricket match when Graham was trying to watch football; Albert admitted he was to blame as he'd always loved cricket.

I advised Graham and Diane to talk to Albert as they would to anyone who was staying in their home, asking for certain things to be respected. Albert has responded well to this and continues to be a beneficial influence in the house, so they consider he must have been a decent chap when he was alive. As I pointed out to them both—when we die we retain the same personality traits, character and sense of humour that we had when still in a physical body. And dogs, obviously, continue their old tricks too!

Diane was so intrigued by the story of Albert that she decided to search for historical evidence of him and eventually found him listed in the local census records as having lived at their address many years ago. When Graham and Diane asked the landlady why she hadn't told them the flat was haunted she replied that if she made it known she would never be able to lease the flat.

Albert also told me that on one occasion before Graham and Diane had moved in, he had seen off a burglar who had one leg over the windowsill when Albert materialised before him to scare him off. This was verified by the landlady, she had been told of it by the local police who had arrested the burglar and charged him with a number of offences. He admitted to them that he had tried to burgle the landlady's property, but had been terrified by the appearance of a ghost and had scarpered.

I had told Graham that Albert's favourite composer was Chopin, so he went out and purchased a CD of Chopin's music for Albert's enjoyment, as well as recording cricket matches for Albert on the VCR. Graham said they often went out leaving an apparently empty flat with Chopin playing or a cricket match playing on the TV!

Here is a testimonial I received from Diane . . .

"After listening to Susan's explanation of the events we had experienced, we were able to accept and understand what had happened. After a long discussion with Susan, and to the amazement of others, we decided as long as Albert abides by the rules and doesn't frighten us at nights, we will let him stay and not ask Susan to send him over. Certain friends and family are sceptical about visiting us, knowing we have a resident spirit! We would like to thank Susan for her help after so many other, so-called professional clairvoyants were not willing to help us."

Chapter 40

To tell you something about being a medium, of what it is like to have communication with deceased people, the best way I can describe the ability is that I hear voices. Not so many years ago people could be dragged kicking and screaming to an asylum for daring to say they could hear voices, so it is with some relief that we are in the 21st century. When I say that I hear voices, it is not like a direct voice in my ear—although occasionally it can be, and when this happens it's marvellous—but what clairaudience (clear hearing) actually is for me, is hearing a voice in my consciousness. I am aware that someone is trying to break into my thoughts so I let them.

Obviously if this happens in a check out queue it's a little inconvenient but I still listen, as in one case where I was asked to give a message to a lady further along in the queue. I was stood there patiently waiting to pay for my groceries thinking of nothing other than what to make for tea when I felt a young woman was trying to get through to me, so I asked her, in my mind, what she wanted.

"I want you to give a message to my mum,"

Great, I thought, now I have to accost a stranger in the supermarket. Again!

"That's my mum in the blue coat"

"Ok," I said, "but it better be good and I want detail before I accost anyone."

"It's my birthday today, I'm twenty-six. Mum put yellow chrysanthemums on my grave this morning."

"Ok, that's lovely but what else, what's the message?"

"Tell her the insurance document she's looking for has curled itself over the back of the dresser drawer in the kitchen—she didn't pull the drawer out far enough." By this time the lady in the blue coat was through the checkout and I was being served.

"Stay with me." I mentally said to the young woman, while paying for and packing my groceries and trying to keep the lady in the blue coat in view.

"Hurry." she said.

Have you ever tried to chat politely to the cashier, hurry to pay for and pack groceries, and keep eye on someone's whereabouts and listen to a 'dead' person? It's not easy! Groceries in hand, I began to hurry down through the store, the lady in the blue coat was almost at the door. I mentally told her daughter to be ready because I was going to stop her mother, and I wasn't doing this alone. I heard her laugh and then I stopped her mother.

"Excuse me," I said, she looked at me blankly, "I'm really sorry to bother you, I'm a medium. Do you know what that is?"

"Yes," she said warily, although drawing some comfort from the fact that I looked reasonably normal. I then told her what I had heard in the queue.

The lady was emotional, but said that it was her daughters 26th birthday, that she had taken yellow chrysanthemums to the cemetery that morning, and yes, she was looking for an insurance document. Phew!

She took my number and promised to ring me if she found the document where her daughter said it was, because I was as intrigued as she was. Later that evening I got the call; the document had indeed been curled over the back of the dresser drawer in the kitchen.

Chapter 41

Similar scenarios like this have happened to me so many times I have lost count. In the early days I was often too nervous to approach people, in case I offended anyone or they thought I was a nut case, but I learnt over the years that spirit people would never put me in a position where the message would not be accepted or appreciated. They have been right every time. Now I realise that what is for me a regular occurrence, would at times be life changing for the person I'm speaking to. I am very aware of people's emotional state too, so I made it a rule a long time ago that if someone wanted a message given to someone else, they do the organising.

I would never approach someone with nuggets of perceived wisdom unless I had heard from a spirit person asking me to do so. They call the shots, every single time. And this silliness you sometimes hear *that we shouldn't disturb the dead*—that causes no end of hilarity because *they* do all the disturbing. People who have died are not laying around waiting for the second coming, they're busy watching you getting on with your life, often with a gentle nudging from them; or they're watching you make a hash of something and busting a gut to intervene, to save you from yourself.

What they do the rest of the time I have no idea, but I do know this: people who love you—really love you—know all that you do and all that you want to do, and are behind you cheering you on when you're getting it right; and no doubt slapping their foreheads in despair when you're not. They are people, people no longer in a physical body, that's all. Not entities, not ghosts, not spooks, not lost, not ghouls, not spectres of lord knows what else—people, pure and simple. And as such, I offer them the same respect I would someone in a physical body.

I also occasionally, physically see people who have died too, and that let me tell you is an awesome experience; although this doesn't happen nearly as much as I would like it to. Most of the seeing takes place in my mind, on a different level of consciousness than my everyday mind. This ability is known as clairvoyance (clear seeing) which makes it sound a lot less complicated than it really is. Most of the time I see images in my mind—places—people, but occasionally a spirit person actually shows up. Despite what you may have read or seen in some dubious television programmes, they don't wander around in a white sheet making 'whoo-whoo' noises. If you are lucky enough to see a full materialisation, as it's called, you will see a person who is often semi transparent. But they can and do communicate, and what blows me away every time is that when they touch you, they feel solid and warm. Lord knows what physics would make of that; but then scientists say the bumblebee shouldn't be able to fly although it clearly does so very well—so they don't know everything. No-one knows everything. I have no idea how half of the things I experience happen to me, I just accept that they do and that it's always for the good; I am happy with that.

Being a medium—and this just means a mediator between those who have ostensibly died and those who haven't—is not an easy path. And I'm sure is not one a lot of people would choose if they knew of the amount of prejudice, bigoted thinking and sheer disbelief that they are likely to encounter from people who don't wish to avail themselves of an informed opinion. I realise there are people out there who abuse what ability they have, and shame on them. Being a medium is not about power, it's not about being holier-than-thou, it's not about ego, manipulation or greed—it's about truth and love and compassion.

Sadly there are those for whom the edges have blurred, and scaring people into parting with money and peace of mind is their stock in trade; but they will come to a sticky end, they always do. Granted, we sometimes have to wait a while to see it, but it comes. So if you ever visit a medium that has an inflated sense of their own importance, who tells you things that scare you—you are in the wrong place. Leave whilst your sanity is still intact. But if you visit a medium who is able to tell you things which were only known by yourself and someone who has died, who is able to give you proof that your loved ones are communicating—then rest easy. You are in a good place. Any visit to a medium should leave you uplifted, empowered and with peace of mind, knowing those who love you are watching over you and loving you still.

I don't know what it's like to not hear, see and feel things about situations and people: to me it's like breathing; but although I'm breathing every minute of every day I'm not talking to 'dead people' all the time. I have a normal life—you will find me having to clean the bathroom like everyone else—the only difference is sometimes I'm not alone when I'm doing it. Now if someone coming through was to wipe a duster around my lounge every now and then it would be a bonus, but as I've said, it's in our quiet moments that spirit people come through, so if you want to develop an ability which is already within all of us, if you want to learn how to communicate with those you love, you must make time.

Make a quiet time to do so—not in the ad breaks between your favourite programmes—set a time once or twice a week where you will turn off every distracting device in the house, and then talk out loud to someone you love. They will hear you, of that you can be absolutely certain. Less certain is whether they can reply to you, but if for instance, you have asked for help with a problem, they will guide you to someone who has the answer, and if over the following days, the name of a particular medium keeps coming to mind over and over, or you keep hearing his or her name being mentioned then make an appointment, because someone you love is trying to reach you with detailed advice.

If however, you are serious about learning how to use this ability which we all have—ask around in your area; word of mouth is the best recommendation for someone who teaches the development of mediumship. It takes time, years in fact, to be able to understand the mechanisms of it, but truly it is easier than you think. Don't pay out shed loads of money to someone who only has half an idea, and usually a barmy one at that. These are people you are learning to communicate with—they are not in the slightest bit interested in odd rituals, you definitely keep your clothes on, and you do not need enough crystals to sink a battleship. You only need your mind, and bucket-loads of common sense.

So, you are talking to people—granted these are people you can't see yet but they will be listening—the difficult bit however is getting them to reply to you. Then when they do reply, you have to be able to understand what they're saying; work out if they are who they say they are, if they're telling the truth.

When you endeavour to start doing readings (I have no idea why giving messages is called a reading, because you don't read anything—definitely not their mind which is just as well in some cases!) not only must you consider all of the above, but also work out whether the person you are about to astonish with your new found talent actually wants to hear from their Uncle Peter, who was the bane of their life when he was alive.

More importantly than that, how do you prove to the poor unfortunate, who has by now adopted a 'rabbit caught in headlights', expression that you are genuine, and not on day release from the local mental institution? The best thing is to look normal—that takes care of the element of surprise—then when you do impart some nugget of wisdom that only they and Uncle Peter knew, the prospective client is so astonished and impressed, that the second coming couldn't have had greater impact.

One thing you must not assume is that it's easy for spirit people to contact us: spirit people have to be taught to communicate. Some are very sloppy at it and expect the lowly medium to just know what they're getting at, after what feels like an eternity to the struggling medium, the contact tails off because the spirit person hasn't got their act together—but it's the medium that ends up feeling foolish. A sufficiently experienced medium will have known immediately that they'd got a tenuous connection, and will be mentally telling the spirit person to pull their finger out.

The most important thing to remember is that spirit people are just that—people, with all their faults and failings still firmly in place. Think about it, if your brother is coming through in a reading and he always swore like a trooper, wouldn't it make sense in terms of identification that he still did so? If you had a sanitised version of your brother's message, you wouldn't be truly convinced it was him. Don't kid yourself that as soon as they die people are absolved of all their annoying foibles and prejudices—far from it, it takes a long time to do that and frankly, for some people, there would never be long enough.

The key to good contact with spirit people is to be relaxed, not to the point of coma, but nice and comfortable, opening your mind to infinite possibilities—and trying not to wonder if you turned the cooker off. Initiating spirit contact is easy; whether they want to have contact with you is less certain. When we send our thoughts out into the ether, it is as though we are sending mail to spirit people. It's easy to imagine messenger angels at the gates clutching piles of our thoughts, prayers, pleadings and offers of deals with God—running through the corridors of heaven shouting "incoming mail, incoming mail!" There will be mail for celestial beings, angels, lesser angels and saints—St Jude, patron saint of lost causes, and advocate of the benefits of Prozac, I'm sure always has a bag full, and doesn't always look pleased to receive it.

The celestial beings such as Michael, (pronounced Micha-el, the el meaning of God), are far too busy to interact with lesser mortals. Besides they're always trailing clouds of glory, which in the spirit world is fine but down here it would be like the glare of a 1000 watt bulb—a light too bright for comfort which would make it difficult to hide imperfections of the spirit. Michael, for those of you who are unsure, is an Archangel; this, to the layman, means that he has the ear of God. That's not to say that God is wandering around with only one ear; no, it just means that whenever Mike wants a word with the big guy, he doesn't have to wait in line like us and everyone else.

A lot of people see Michael as a quicker route to God, obviously hoping he will put in a good word, which if it were true would be great. But all Mike's mail gets dealt with by a whole army of 'little Mikes', who get to open the mail and decide what has priority, and what needs to be sent down the line to other departments—a bit like the civil service, but with personalities. Michael is too busy saving the world to be able to answer a plea for enough money to buy the designer shoes you saw in the sale. One of the other Mikes would open that, show everyone else, they'd all fall about laughing, and then chuck it in the nearest bin.

If an important message came in for say, your dad, then your message would be taken directly to him within seconds of you sending it. The messenger would shuffle his feet for a minute or two while your dad digested it, then enquire if he would like to reply right away, later or if at all. Some messages don't require an answer, but for those who do want to reply there is Heaven's equivalent of the switchboard.

As you might imagine, this is rather alarmingly huge in comparison to one run by your average telephone exchange. Your dad would have to speak to an operator, and she would tell him to start memorizing his message because when his time came to communicate he'd better have it ready—after all, she hadn't got all day, and there were three million other people who wanted to get through.

The operator would then tut to herself: raise her eyebrows in exasperation, moan that everyone takes her for granted, that she ought to have a medal doing this job day after day; and then she'd set about finding a decent medium who could understand your dad's message. If she couldn't find a suitable medium within her remit she'd yell across to her friend Maureen and ask her to see if she had anyone in her area who might look as though they could successfully string two words together.

That done, all that remained would be to give you the impulse to visit a medium, hopefully you'd pick the one they were aiming you at, because here's the rub—you think you are in charge, which causes no end of hilarity in the heavenly realms. You would keep hearing about a particular medium, their name would keep cropping up in conversations all over the place and at unlikely times—for instance, your dentist and his assistant discussing the medium whilst delving about in your root canal, so you'd have no option but to listen and for the idea to lodge in your consciousness—very clever. You would eventually pick up the phone, make an appointment with that medium and a message to that effect would instantly be relayed to your dad who could then begin to panic in earnest about getting his message through to that medium and so by extension, to you.

Think about it—people in spirit form do not have a physical body, so they don't have a brain, as such, to carry all the information around that they used to. But they do have a spirit mind; all communication with spirit takes place by thought alone. Your dad will draw upon the emotions that are most powerful to him, mainly his love for you. And he will also get around to letting you know that he knows your mother binned his beloved train set after he died, but did she realise that it would have fetched a mint on eBay. The fact that your poor mother had it on her dining table for the last thirty years, and missed vital moments of Coronation Street every time the whistle blew would have entirely escaped him—her heaving it into the bin with a passion would have helped her grieving process no end.

Your dad would have to hold the thoughts and memories in his mind that he wanted to get to you, then beam them at the medium, who hopefully could hear and see them in her mind and then pass the information on to you clearly—no easy feat!

Chapter 42

In my experience, when people pass into spirit form they jettison all information that is no longer of any use or interest to them, only information that has emotional content is deemed worth keeping. The only reason people in spirit form communicate in the first place is to try to put your mind at rest, by letting you know they are fine, giving you advice about a problem and telling you that you are loved. Some spirit people are a bit hesitant with the love bit, usually because saying it didn't come easy to them when they were alive, or because they were an absolute pig to you and in a fit of conscience want to make amends.

Whether you want to accept that is entirely up to you, and sadly forgiveness can be a bit of a grey area—it is a very personal thing and most people don't do it very well . . . dead or alive. So for future reference it might be a good idea to tidy up loose ends before you shuffle off this mortal coil, otherwise you will find yourself trying to tell a medium that you want forgiveness from your sister for telling her boyfriend she was seeing his friend as well—something you had vehemently denied for the last forty years. Or that you're sorry for keeping your mother's favourite ring when you know it should have gone to your sister.

And here's the rub—those who have died know exactly what was done with their possessions. When you arrive in the heavenly realms you want your mum to be pleased to see you, not armed with a list of questions as to why you gave her watch to your aunt when they hadn't spoken for years, and why did you sell her silver and keep the money when she had left instructions that it was to be given to her favourite cats home. Be assured, they know *everything!*

A prime example of this was a lady who arranged a reading with me. She arrived with a young man: they seemed nice enough and the reading got underway. Within seconds I was aware of a very angry young man coming through, and he was refusing to talk to me. I mentally asked him what the problem was.

"She's my mother but I don't want to talk to her"

"Why not?" I asked

"She's been through my stuff!" Then he showed me an image of a house that looked as though it had been ransacked.

I said to the woman in front of me, "I have a man here who is very angry with you. He tells me you're his mother but he doesn't want to speak to you because you have ransacked his house"

Her face was a picture of disbelief and the young man beside her squirmed so much you'd have thought he had worms. I went on to describe a wardrobe he was showing me and a blue box which was empty. He tells me you were looking for his will and thought you'd found it in a blue box but when you forced it open it was empty—more squirming.

The man came through again. "She wants my money but she didn't even bring me up"

I relayed this to the woman, who reluctantly admitted she hadn't brought this son up, but as he'd died she felt she was entitled to his considerable assets because she gave birth to him. I hid my feelings rather well, considering—something else you have to do as a medium, personal feelings cannot be allowed to come into a reading.

I allowed the man coming through to say more. "Tell her, she's not having anything. I left a will but it isn't there." He went on to show me just what he did own and asked me to tell his younger brother (the young man) that he loved him, that he would be ok and a sister would be ok, but the others would get nothing. Relaying information is sometimes not easy, but as a medium, you must say exactly what is said to you. The mother was thoroughly annoyed at being thwarted and threatened to challenge the will.

"I have tied it up," he said, very angry now. "I have tied it up: if she challenges it they all lose, I knew she'd do this."

I relayed this nugget and watched her face fall. Exit a thoroughly annoyed woman! Her son shook my hand and thanked me, saying that he felt bad for helping her go through the flat. I told him his brother knew he was coerced, it's ok.

So you see? They do know *everything*. Something for all of us to think about.

Chapter 43

Something else people in spirit form are good at is manoeuvring the medium into a situation without telling them why—I am so used to this now that it doesn't faze me in the least. Two years ago I was in my local town having done some shopping and thinking about heading home when I heard in my head, "Go back into Marks and Spencer's" (a popular store, great food!)

"Why?" I said.

"Go back into Marks and Spencer's," was the only reply.

Knowing better than to ignore the voice I duly went back into the store with no idea where in the store I was supposed to go. I was wandering aimlessly about, waiting for something to happen when I heard, "Go to the lingerie section." So off I went to lingerie, trying not to look like a shoplifter.

I was idly examining a dressing gown which I didn't want or need, when a woman, a complete stranger, asked me to help her. I looked around and realised it was me she was talking to.

"Of course," I said, "how can I help you?"

This was a Saturday, the shop was very busy and I knew she hadn't confused me with a member of staff because I had my coat on. The lady, clearly emotionally fragile, said she had recently come out of hospital and needed some help buying a few things, as she was staying at a friend's for the weekend. I saw she had a nightdress in her basket and asked if she had a dressing gown—no she didn't, so I helped her to choose a dressing gown to go with her choice nightdress, then slippers, then a wash bag to keep her bits and pieces in. That done, I asked her why she had asked me to help her.

"I don't know," she said, "it was like I was pulled over to you." This was no surprise to me. I explained that I was a medium, and asked did she know what that was?

"Yes," she said. "My daughter was killed a week ago." Bingo! That lady had been led to me in the store because I would understand her need. To cap it off, in my peripheral vision I saw another woman hurrying towards us.

"I don't believe it," she said, getting her breath back. "I'm sorry I'm late, but this is Susan! This is the medium I was telling you about."

The spirit people helping this lady with her pain had known her friend was going to be late, had seen I was in the town and made me go back into the shop, made her speak to me so she would be safe, knowing that I would help her until her friend arrived—very, very clever.

Chapter 44

I was half watching a late film on television one night when I clearly heard a child's voice. At first I thought it was one of my own children already in bed and went to check on them, but everyone was fast asleep. I reasoned that one of them must have called out in their sleep, and settled down again to watch the television.

Suddenly there was the voice again, but this time I was aware that I was hearing clairaudiently. The fact that no-one else in the room appeared to hear anything untoward added weight to my realization. I listened intently as a little girl's insistent voice said over and over, "Ring my dad, ring my dad!"

I explained inwardly that I didn't know who her dad was or even who she was. Instantly her face appeared in my consciousness.

"See" she said, "you do know me. I'm Stephanie."

Indeed I did know her, or at least knew of her. Stephanie had attended the same primary school as my eldest daughter, Claire. I knew then that Stephanie had heart problems, but as we had moved to the other side of town two years previously, I had no idea that she had subsequently died following complicated heart surgery. She must have been around nine when she passed over.

I sat there stunned, and then inwardly explained in the best way I could that it was difficult to phone someone I didn't know, and announce I had a message from their child who had died. The family's grief would have been so raw, and I was terribly worried that I might upset them further. I had no idea what their religious beliefs were either—God forbid that I should offend them in that quarter as well. I was able to come up with countless reasons why I shouldn't telephone her parents.

Stephanie seemed to accept this quite calmly and the moment passed. It was as though she had gone away to digest this and find a way around it, allowing me to return to the film. But I was now unsettled and ended up pacing around the house knowing a way had to be found around this situation, because I knew with absolute certainty that I would be hearing from Stephanie again.

The next evening she was back with a mission. She was going to keep on at me until I phoned her dad. Insistent—this child could win a prize for tenacity and sheer will power. She had found the right 'wavelength' in communicating with me and was going to use it until I gave in. Over the next few days I was unable to read a book, watch television, do household chores or even go shopping without hearing Stephanie's voice repeating over and over again.

"Ring my dad, ring my dad." She wasn't distressed in any way—just very, very insistent.

I puzzled over this dilemma—I wanted to help her but I definitely did not want to add to her parent's distress; while I puzzled this out, Stephanie just kept on.

Finally, unable to stand the onslaught any longer, I said to her, "All right, all right, I give in. I'll ring your dad." Stephanie, clearly delighted to have won the day, became excited. I shot up a quick prayer asking for help in dealing with this tricky situation. While scouring the phone book for her parent's telephone number I said to her, "You'd better tell me something only your parents will know, I have to convince them that it is you talking to me"

The little girl told me of her favourite toy, a rabbit, that had been placed in her coffin, and of the bridesmaids dress she had been buried in. I agonized over making the call and actually went to the phone, picked it up, began to dial and then chickened out several times. Then, filled with trepidation, I picked up the phone and forced myself to dial the number. The phone seemed to ring for ages, and then I heard a man's voice answer. Stephanie was leaping up and down with sheer excitement, shouting.

"It's my dad, it's my dad."

Mentally I asked her to pipe down so I could hear myself think—I began a faltering conversation. I introduced myself, and in one breath spoke of knowing the family through the junior school and how much I didn't want to upset them, but I was psychic and had been hearing Stephanie.

Silence.

"Oh God!" I thought, "I've blown it."

"My rabbit," I heard Stephanie, "mention my rabbit."

"You see," I stumbled, "the thing is, she told me about a toy rabbit that was placed in her coffin, and the bridesmaids dress she was wearing."

The silence seemed to go on forever, and then he said, "When can you come to the house?"

I nearly dropped on the spot with sheer relief, while Stephanie was bursting with excitement, obviously pleased that I had done as she had asked.

"See," she said "I told you dad would listen."

The next evening I followed the directions to the family home, acutely aware of Stephanie's presence all the way. I chatted to her during the journey.

"Right then, Lady Jane—you set this up so you better stick with me, help me out here, don't desert me now."

The door was opened by Malcolm, Stephanie's dad, who was obviously wary, but friendly all the same. He led me into a very smart lounge to meet Carol, Stephanie's mum. I needn't have worried about being nervous, when I began explaining how much Stephanie was pestering me they both laughed and said she was like that. She'd go on and on until she had been heard—tenacious was an understatement.

Stephanie's presence seemed to fill the room as she communicated with me.

"Tell mum I saw all the flowers at the funeral—some looked like toys and my Nan gave me flowers in the shape of a skipping rope" She went on to describe a favourite party dress—she especially liked the lace collar and the flouncy skirt and the fact that it was a greeny blue colour.

Then she suddenly said, "Tell dad to get the biscuit tin."

As I sat there a bit puzzled, Malcolm rushed off and returned with the tin—it wasn't full of biscuits but full of photographs. He tipped them onto the floor where he excitedly sifted through them. In triumph he held up a photograph of Stephanie in a greeny blue taffeta dress, complete with flounces and a lace collar.

We sat for several hours as Stephanie, via myself, regaled her parents with information about family occasions she was aware of, wanting them to know she had shared in those times despite the lack of her physical presence. She told me that her younger brother's room had been decorated, that he had changed beds and also had a new duvet cover. Stephanie also said her brother had reported seeing her in his room, but when he had said so to his mum and dad they thought he had been dreaming. Stephanie wanted them to know that he had seen her. She spoke of an aunty who had recently had a baby and of many, many things personal to the family. It was midnight before we finished talking, surrounded by photographs. Stephanie was beginning to tire by this stage, but was contented that she had been able to let her parents know that she was safe and well.

The amount of evidence given by Stephanie proved to them, beyond all doubt that she was still around, and I was grateful to be able to make the loss of their daughter's presence just that little more bearable. As she said farewell at the door, Carol said it was the mention of the toy rabbit that had convinced them I was real, because only they and Stephanie knew it had been placed in her coffin.

Chapter 45

Just when Anne was getting herself together emotionally and materially after a messy and somewhat unpleasant divorce, she found herself hurtling towards yet another crisis. Already estranged from her daughter and sister, she was trying to hold together the remaining threads of her life and run a business to keep a roof over her head, when she received a devastating phone call.

Anne's mother and father, now retired, had been preparing to move into a bungalow, when her mother died. The news that Anne received was doubly devastating, she was told that following thorough medical checks, both parents had been discovered to have terminal illnesses and had both been given only a short time to live. Just a week before she was due to move into her new home, Anne's mother died.

Coping stoically with her grief, Anne installed a manager to run her thriving business and moved the 200 miles to be nearer to her father. But Pops, as he was affectionately known, lived in the new bungalow for only a short time before moving in with Anne.

It was during this time of grief and anxiety that Anne began to have nagging doubts about her business—there were conflicting reports from colleagues, her calls were not being returned and there were worrying letters from her bank. As Pops became more and more frail, Anne coped as best she could keeping her mounting financial fears to herself.

She heard that clients were leaving her business in droves due to the unprofessional conduct of her landlord, and while her solicitor tried to help, the disappointment and utter dejection were crippling. Anne did her best to salvage what was left of her business but the relentless pressure from her landlord and the bank, coupled with the death of her beloved Pops, culminated in a breakdown of her health. With no-one to support her in any way, she found herself totally alone. The legal problems and chaos, including threats of enforced bankruptcy by the bank, were still rumbling on when she found her way to my door.

As we sat and I began to explain to Anne what can and cannot be expected from a clairvoyant reading, I was immediately aware of an elderly gentleman impatient to talk. At first his presence in my consciousness wasn't so clear. Certainly there was enough for me to know that an elderly man was trying to communicate, but the connection wasn't strong enough for me to hear him properly. This had happened to me before, and I knew that if I relaxed and waited, he might be able to gain the wherewithal to impress information on me much more clearly. Sometimes this situation can best be described as trying to hear someone who is a long way off and talking through plastic sheeting. Not easy at all.

Suddenly he was right there—this elderly gentleman, bright and sharp in my clairvoyant vision with a voice as clear as a bell. By some supreme effort, he had pushed through whatever invisible barrier had previously been in his way. I was impressed, as this was a very determined man; for a first time communicator he was doing very well. I was to find out very soon that it was not only this man's strength of character but also his extreme annoyance which was propelling him forward.

I described the gentleman to Anne who confirmed that this was her father. He talked in a very agitated manner, saying that there were huge problems to do with the business. He said that Anne was in serious trouble due to the landlord's unscrupulous dealings, but that if she did what he told her, then the months of worry, fear and harassment from official bodies would be over in a fortnight.

"Right," he said, "here are my instructions. You have to write to every director of the bank, sending each one copies of the proof you have, detailing the landlords failings. There should be 6 letters explaining everything and 18 copies of evidence." Anne did indeed have proof that VAT totalling thousands of pounds, as well as other crippling amounts of money had been paid by her to the landlord. She left me that night and went home to write the letters as directed by Pops.

Two weeks later, to the day, Anne received a phone call from one of the bank's directors stating that it wasn't the bank's policy to make people like Anne bankrupt. A major burden had been lifted, and Anne was able to concentrate on re-building her life. Pops had been a great influence in Anne's life—he had loved music and sport, had been a passionate gardener all his life, and was proud, thoughtful and compassionate. He wasn't about to let a little thing like being dead prevent him from helping a cherished daughter.

Chapter 46

The deceased people I communicate with look and sound as real to me as you do, so for me, they are people—no two ways about it—but, for the sake of this story I will refer to them as spirit so as not to confuse with those who still inhabit a physical body.

Stuart had decided that enough was enough and had moved into his brother's bedroom. He was refusing to sleep in his room again until something was done about 'it'—'it' being what he believed to be a ghost.

Someone or something was seriously freaking Stuart out. Doors would open by themselves, his CD player would switch itself on then switch itself off, and he would wake up in the night with the intense feeling that someone else was in the room. The rest of the family often felt as though they were being followed around the house and most scary of all, footsteps were regularly heard walking along the passage and they always stopped outside Stuart's room.

His brother, Daniel, had also felt his duvet being tugged, and their mother, Helen, had often found the kettle boiling away merrily to itself, and once she had woken in the night to feel someone leaning over her. Understandably, the family were at their wits end when I received a call from Helen, and arranged to visit the family the following evening.

I arrived the next night, at a cosy bungalow on the outskirts of the town. The family appeared a little nervous at what I might be about to do. If they had been expecting some kind of ritual they were to be disappointed—I'd brought along nothing but myself and a hefty dose of common sense.

Very few spirit people are hostile—they may well be annoyed, but so would you be if you couldn't make yourself heard or understood after repeated and increasingly desperate efforts. After asking each member of the family to tell me their experiences, I could tell from their descriptions and the atmosphere in the house that we weren't dealing with anything nasty. I began a tour of the various rooms accompanied by Helen and her son Stuart, to find out who was causing all the fuss.

When I walk around a haunted property, if I haven't already seen the spirit person as I've entered the house, I will go from room to room looking for activity, and by this I mean a feeling like an electrical charge running through my body. It starts at my feet and sweeps through my whole body in waves—this happens when I walk in and out of an energy field which is produced by a spirit person in order to appear here and hopefully communicate. Sometimes it is no more than every hair on my body standing on end magnified ten times over, but on other occasions the electrical charge is so strong that it feels as though a television could be run off it for a week.

Helen and David's room was calm . . . so no spirits in there. Next was eldest son, Daniel's room and I could tell from the level of energy in the room that a spirit person had been visiting, and was a young male, but that was it. Next was Stuart's room, just from putting my hand on the door knob I knew this room was absolutely humming with spirit activity.

I entered the room followed by Helen, and her son Stuart, and was immediately consumed within a very intense energy field, so much so that my entire body began shaking internally. In my experience this happens because the spirit person knows they can communicate with me—their excitement at this realisation creates even more of this electrical energy, which in turn sets up a tremor within my energy field, or aura as some people know it. I am aware that only I know the tremor is in place—the last thing I want is the people I'm helping to think I'm scared.

I told the family we had company, and Stuart was immediately and understandably nervous. I explained that nothing frightening was going to happen, I was just going to have a chat with a dead man. Within seconds I was hearing the very excited voice of a young man. I had to ask him to calm down, so that I could hear him clearly and be able to pass on what he wanted to say. The atmosphere in the room was so charged that the family could feel it themselves, and there was more than enough energy zapping about to run a small substation for a fortnight.

This young man told me he had been a close friend of the family: he told me his name was Jono, and endless details about himself that only the family would know, to verify that it was him. He explained that he had died very suddenly as a result of an accident. He said where on his body he had been affected and wanted his family to know that he hadn't felt a thing—he had passed out before he fell and hit his head. He was very matter of fact about it and demonstrated to me that it was as quick as putting a light out. He knew he had been taken to hospital because he went along to have a look, but there was nothing medically that could have been done for him.

He apologised for scaring the family—that hadn't been his intention. He said he had been trying to get their attention for some time but couldn't make himself understood.

Jono began talking in earnest, wanting to warn Stuart about his amplifier leads. He said they were in a dodgy state and would cause a fire if it wasn't sorted. Stuart pulled out the leads to his amplifier and showed us that Jono was right: they were in a decidedly dangerous condition. He was so shocked that Jono should know this and warn him that he agreed to get new leads instead of making do.

Jono went on to talk about Stuarts considerable musical talent, telling him that his band would be successful, and that the singer who had recently quit still wanted to be in the band, but wanted to be in the background—he was worried that the others might not want him because he didn't want to sing. Stuart confirmed this information to be true.

At this point Helen's husband, David, came into the room and contact with Jono was interrupted as another voice broke into the conversation. The owner of this voice was also male, he said he was called Richard and had been a friend of David's, who had died when he was shot by a sniper whilst driving an army vehicle full of soldiers. He'd managed to pull the vehicle off the road to safety and stop, before he'd died. A shocked David confirmed this to be true.

Richard went on to say that David was having a lot of pain in his hands, left hand especially, and if he was to massage olive oil into his hands every night he would be fine; if not his hands would stiffen up and become too painful to work with. David, who's eyes were now like organ stops, said that was really odd because he did have painful hands, and the other night he had been in the kitchen and didn't know why but had felt a strong compulsion to rub olive oil into his hands. He had done so, and found that they were all the better for it.

I explained that, in my experience, if a spirit person couldn't make themselves seen or heard to whoever they wanted to communicate with, they will try to guide you through your gut instinct and you'd think it was all your idea.

The evening came to a satisfactory conclusion—Richard had wanted to be remembered to David and to pass on the tip about his hands. As the conversation with Richard ended, Jono popped back to let everyone know he was very fond of them and thanked them all for their friendship over the years. He knew he was missed by the family, so it had been important to him to let them know he was absolutely fine and was still a part of their lives as he had always been. This was tremendously comforting for the family who had been very shocked and upset at his early and tragic death, and Jono was pretty chuffed with himself at having made contact and doing it so well.

I have increasingly found that spirit people who love you will make every effort in any way they can to get your attention—they do hear the thoughts you send to them, they know when they are missed and can feel the emotion as keenly as you do. If there is any way at all in which they can impress their thoughts or feelings or presence upon you, be it days, months or years after their death, they will do so. That, in my experience, is guaranteed.

CHAPTER 47

Many people have asked me, "How do I *really know* that the people I love in spirit can see me?" I can do no better than recount for you an evening some years ago.

I was quietly watching television one evening when I became aware of my friend's parents in my consciousness. I asked if they wanted me to pass on a message they said yes, and waved.

I said, "Is that it?"

"Yes." they said.

Slightly baffled, I rang my friend Scilla. "I've just had your mum and dad here"

"Oh great, did they have anything to say?" Scilla asked.

"No Scilla, they just waved at you."

I then heard my friend burst into tears. When she recovered herself, she explained that the night before she had been missing her parents very badly and had gone into her lovely garden and waved at the midnight sky saying, "I love you Mum, I love you Dad."

And if you need further proof . . .

Three years ago I was asked to visit a local Hospice: a gentleman there had heard of me and asked to see me. I went straight away, and was shown into a room—I shook hands with John who was very ill with cancer. When I entered his room I was immediately aware of a lady stood at the back of the room watching me. She was holding a glass of whisky, and smiled at me as I acknowledged her and mentally asked who she was. John asked me if I could see anyone else in the room. I replied that there was a lady with us who told me she was his mum.

She said, "Come on John, you're holding up the party!"

John smiled broadly and said he had been seeing his mum for several days. He had wanted to see if I could see her, then he would know it was real and not the drugs he was taking. He asked when she was going to take him. I asked her.

She replied, "At 6am tomorrow."

I told John and he said, "You tell her I'm ready."

John passed from this life at 6am the following morning.

Someone will come for you. When it is your time to leave this physical world, someone you love and who loves you will come for you. No-one, no matter how or in what circumstances, ever leaves this world alone.

Chapter 48

So you see, my life has, so far, been full of many and varied experiences of communicating with what, to all intents and purposes, are deceased people. I have never been afraid—your own imagination can scare you far more than any spirit person would ever intend to do. The thing is to be relaxed about it all, you are only communicating with people after all. What can possibly be complicated about that? We communicate with people every day; it shouldn't be any different just because they are not inhabiting a physical body.

Granted, it can make you jump when you meet someone on the landing when you have gone for a wee in the middle of the night, but they're only coming because they know you're awake and therefore easy to communicate with, because the television or CD player isn't going at full tilt. After being scared in such a way one night a long time ago, and only just making it to the toilet, I made it a rule then that no-one was to visit me like that, and then they never have since. You're talking to people, and they will, for the most part, be respectful, but what you must do is make time the next day so they can come to you. After all, they are making a huge effort so it would be rude not to.

The first specific meeting with a spirit person, or rather the hearing of one, that I can clearly remember was when I was coming up to eleven years old. We lived in a lovely big house which had an orchard at the back, in a village near Stratford upon Avon. On this particular day my brothers were climbing trees in the orchard and as I was bored I decided to go and annoy them as only sisters can.

My brothers began goading me—you know the usual 'girls can't climb trees' stuff. I, in my wisdom, decided to show them I could, and began to climb the tree—the biggest one in the orchard. I figured if they could do it, so could I; that was my first mistake.

I climbed as high up as I could. Then my brothers shinned down the tree and left me there; they ran off howling in delight that I was now firmly wedged, almost at the very top of this very tall tree. I was immediately panic stricken because, in my haste to prove them wrong, I hadn't given a single thought to how I was going to get down.

Mistake number two—the more I panicked, the more the tree swayed. I was too far from the house for my mother to hear, besides she wasn't going to climb the tree to get me down; and my dad, who would have, was at work. Every time I looked down the tree swayed and I just knew I was perilously close to falling out of it. I wrapped my arms around a branch and literally froze with fear.

I don't know how long I was like this, probably only a few minutes, when I heard a voice—a male voice, very calming and very serious.

He said, "If you listen to me you will get down safely." I wasn't going to risk looking down again to see who was in the orchard. I was just grateful someone was prepared to help me.

"Put your hands here, put your feet here." he said. I did as I was told and have no memory of my descent other than finding myself on the grass beneath the tree.

I looked around—there was no-one in sight. I don't recall thinking this was odd in the least, and raced off to punish my brothers for leaving me in the tree.

Looking back this was probably my first conscious memory of 'hearing' people, and because it didn't freak me out in the slightest I had probably been unconsciously hearing spirit people for some time before that.

I now know that the voice belonged to Ethan—a spirit guide who has worked with me ever since; and who has probably been driven insane with my stubbornness over the years but has stayed with me nonetheless. His advice has always been correct and has saved me from myself and others many times, and as I said earlier, I figured that anyone who was prepared to do that must be all good, and so it has proved.

I was thirty-two when it occurred to me to ask him to physically turn up in person. I have no idea why I waited so long, probably because I had been seeing him in my head and hearing him for so long, I knew he was real enough. But this day I said to him that it would be lovely if he would turn up sometime and thought no more about it.

Around two weeks later I woke in the night: I lay there wondering if I needed to use the toilet, like you do, when I became aware that someone was stood beside my bed. I turned my head and there he was—almost as solid as you or I! I remember noticing that I could see the pattern of my curtains through his robe. He looked just the same as he had in my head all these years and I was absolutely awestruck.

He smiled at me and held out his hands as if to say, "Here I am". All I could do was lay there and stare at him—I could feel the love coming from him, nothing like love as we know it . . . stronger, unconditional. I couldn't think of a single coherent thing to say except "'Thank you, thank you, thank you" then he faded from view.

I lay awake for ages, and knowing he can hear me I told him that if I never saw him again like that until I die then that was enough. Now scientists will tell you that this was a hallucination—this from people who have never had a spiritual experience—but I can tell you he was real; awesomely, amazingly real. No matter what anyone could say to the contrary I know this as an absolute irrefutable truth.

Everyone, he tells me, has a guide; and when they start to walk the path of inner development they will become known to them. As you are reading this book, you must have an interest in this path yourself. Because of free will, spirit people cannot intervene in our lives, but you can try asking your guide to show up—they may do so very quickly or you may wait years. If you are serious about learning to help others, and they know if you are or not, at sometime, when you are ready, they will show up.

Even if you don't want to go as far as hearing or seeing spirit people you can still chat to people you love, they hear you, of that you can be absolutely certain. I remember a lady coming to me for a reading a long time ago, her mum came through and gave evidence to her daughter that only she knew, to prove this even further she said her daughter had been leaning against the kitchen sink at 5am on Tuesday morning, she was holding blue mug full of tea, having a few tears and had asked aloud for her mum to help her with a specific problem. Her mum outlined the problem (but as that is private, you don't need to know that bit), the client, amazed, verified that this was true.

And to prove that people you love who have died know everything . . . a young lady came to see me who was hoping for contact with her mum. Her mum duly came through and the reading went well but as the young lady was about to leave her mum asked me to give her a piece of rose quartz in the shape of a heart that I had on a bookshelf.

I did so without question saying "Your mum wants you to have this."

She burst into tears as I put it in her hands and said her mum had given her one before she died and she'd lost it. Amazing eh?

It blows me away every time something like this happens, and I've been this way for *years*.

CHAPTER 49

THE NUN

I have been enormously privileged to have been a medium, through which these remarkable people have been able to lend their voices. I hope I did them proud. To conclude, here is my personal story to bring both hope and a quiet certainty that no matter how wretched your life appears to be, you are being looked after. All you have to do is trust . . .

When I was twenty-three I was going through a very unhappy time in my marriage and was in great distress. With lots of worries about money, two small children to take care of, I was feeling as though I had no support from my husband. I felt as though I was trying to hold everything together on my own.

This particular evening had been no different from any other: I prayed as usual for some help, some guidance. I remember I had been sobbing for a while, and then eventually fell asleep. I must have fallen asleep sitting up when something woke me—I was wide awake and lay there wondering why I'd woken.

It was very dark outside so I thought it was the early hours of the morning. As I lay there against the pillows I listened for any noises from the children's bedroom; I noticed that my bedroom was getting lighter and lighter, a bright light that felt comforting and didn't alarm me in the least.

As the light began to fill the room I noticed my bedroom door opening at the same time. At first I thought it was my eldest daughter, who was four at the time, coming to get in with me for a cuddle, something she often did if she woke up. As I watched the door open, I realised it wasn't my daughter coming in, it was a nun; I was transfixed by this but not afraid at all. I watched her walk over to my side of the bed and sit down: I felt the bed give under her just as it would if someone sat on it.

She said, "Give me your hands."

Without question, I did so, her hands were warm and firm. She looked right at me and said I wasn't to worry because some money was coming on Tuesday, and that my husband would have a job the following week.

Then she gave my hands a squeeze, and looking into my eyes, she said I would have a difficult decision to make in the near future, and not to worry because I would make the right choice.

With that, the Nun faded away right before my eyes, as she did so, the room began to darken again. I lay there in absolute wonderment for ages sending up silent 'thank you's until I fell asleep.

The following Tuesday morning there was a cheque on the mat for six hundred pounds—an unexpected tax rebate, and my husband was offered a job the following week. My big decision came two years later when I left the marriage.

In times of great distress or great need, your guides or your family will reach you as best they can. Although they cannot prevent certain lessons which you have to learn, they can guide you through difficult times—letting you know you are loved and looked after, which can make your load and your journey easier to bear.

*I believe I can do no better than to conclude this book with
the following words which I 'heard' one evening...*

<u>Remember</u>

We get to see all the things that are done in our honour—
candles lit for us, prayers, special little ceremonies.
Everything that's consciously done for us,
in memory of us, is known about.
You should know that. Everyone should know that.
It is *so* important to be remembered.
Graves are not as important to us as they are to you.
We don't want you visiting cemeteries in all weathers.
If you want to remember us on special days put a flower
beside a photograph, or better still, light a candle.
The intention behind that tiny light reaches us here
in the spiritual worlds, and brings with it a burst of
intense happiness that we've been remembered.
Sometimes it's the smallest things that carry the most weight.

To my question—whether we might not fortify our minds for the approach of death—he answered in a passion... "No sir, let it alone. It matters not how a man dies, but how he lives. The act of dying is not of importance, it lasts so short a time."

James Boswell: Life of Johnson 1791 (Samuel Johnson 1708-1784)

About the Author

Susan Pengelly lives with her husband, Stephen, in the beautiful region of North Devon, England. She is blessed with four children, four step-children, and at the time of writing, four grandchildren.

Born in December 1960, Susan became aware of her mediumistic and clairvoyant abilities at the age of eleven. She began offering private readings around the age of twenty-one, and continues to do so to this day. She has used her abilities in many fields; notably as a civil celebrant, specialising in funeral ceremonies, a magazine columnist, and most particularly as a teacher of meditation and self-development.

One of her achievements, *The English Psychic Company*, offers development classes for those who wish to learn how to hone any psychic or mediumistic ability they have in a down to earth, common-sense way. Susan also organises regular events including psychic suppers, where her senior students give private readings to clients, who also enjoy a meal while they are waiting. These evenings are a huge success in bringing people together in a social setting, to experience a good quality reading. *The Lighthouse* has long been a passion for Susan—a monthly, spiritual meeting for people who, for reasons of their own, don't feel they fit in within the established church.

Susan is also a co-founder of *Spirit Seeker*, a ground-breaking, no-nonsense company which offers products and services that help to bring about transformation and enlightened thinking. She has developed a system of mind work meditations, available on CD, which enables people to change old thought patterns and conditioning with incredible results.

Susan's focus, underpinning all of these activities, is to give people the means to build their own belief system, and to become more awake in the world. Writing is also a passion for Susan, equalled only by her love of life and the people in it.

Susan is soon to publish another book, The Essential Medium, as well as two novels, and a theatre production of *Satnav For Your Soul* is in the pipeline.

Susan can be contacted through her websites

www.spiritseeker.co.uk

www.susanpengelly.com

A Little Tip From Me

Do not listen to negative people.

Creativity exists within us all; it is an expression of our personality and needs to breathe. Whatever you feel like trying, whether its painting, cooking, sewing, writing, carpentry, developing mediumship or healing— do it, start.

If you put enough emotional content into whatever you do, you will succeed, far beyond your own expectations. Let your personality breathe—be you, no matter who says that you can't do it, that it's no good, that it's not going to work, remember that they don't have the vision that you do—they haven't evolved, because they lack the courage to try.

After all, you don't want to be stood at the pearly gates, and St Peter asks why you didn't try all the things you wanted to, and were capable of. Or he shows you the list of people you could have helped, if only you had tried. Then he shows you how successful you would have been, and how much pleasure it would have given to you, and others.

Too late then, to be gutted; he's likely to put a big cross in the relevant columns, shake his head, and give you a small disappointed smile, as you shuffled through the gates, embarrassed and annoyed at yourself.